D1508818

Psychology
&Theology

Psychology & Theology

Prospects for Integration

Gary R. Collins

edited and with a contribution by
H. Newton Malony

ABINGDON / NASHVILLE

PSYCHOLOGY AND THEOLOGY:
PROSPECTS FOR INTEGRATION

Copyright © 1981 by Abingdon

Library of Congress Cataloging in Publication Data
COLLINS, GARY R.
Psychology and theology.

Composed primarily of lectures given in 1979 as Fuller
Seminary's Ninth Finch Symposium in Psychology and
Religion.
Bibliography: p.
Includes index.
1. Christianity—Psychology. I. Malony, H. Newton. II. Title.
BR110.C6245   261.5'15   81-588

ISBN 0-687-34830-7 (pbk.)   AACR2

MANUFACTURED BY THE PARTHENON PRESS AT
NASHVILLE, TENNESSEE, UNITED STATES OF AMERICA

Contents

Foreword

Early in 1978, Gary Collins delivered the lectures at Fuller Seminary's Ninth Finch Symposium in Psychology and Religion. Those addresses comprise the major part of this volume.

The Finch Symposium was established a decade ago by the faculty of the seminary's Graduate School of Psychology to further the dialogue between the Christian faith and the social/behavioral sciences.

These presentations by Collins are part of a developing tradition of innovative contributions made by such persons as Walter Houston Clark, Richard L. Gorsuch, Thomas A. Oden, Orlo Strunk, Jr., Orville Walters, David B. Myers, and Stanley R. Hopper. They deal with Collins' long-standing concern with the assumptions on which psychology is based, and the application of psychological principles to daily living. His basic conviction is that a psychology built on Christian presuppositions is academically legitimate and behaviorally meaningful.

Responses to Collins' ideas by three faculty members and a doctoral candidate at Fuller Seminary are incorporated into a single chapter by H. Newton Malony. In addition to those of the author, the thoughts of Arthur G. Glasser, Dean of the School of World Mission, Robert N. Schaper, Associate Professor of Preaching, and Timothy Z. Weber, doctoral candidate in clinical psychology, are included.

It is hoped that the publication of these addresses and responses will add significantly to the attempts of many in our day to further the collaboration of religion and science for benefit of all persons and for the glory of God.

H. Newton Malony
Pasadena, California

CHAPTER 1

Integration: The Approaches

Gary R. Collins

Many years ago, when I was a freshman taking a course in general psychology, we were given what to me was a fascinating assignment. All students were required to visit the local mental hospital once a week, to spend an hour or so on the ward, and to bring back a report of what we had learned. This was my first encounter with severe psychological disturbances, and I was both overawed and deeply moved. I also had fun. Some of the patients taught me to play billiards (an activity that wasn't exactly approved of, even at the liberal Baptist university that I was attending), and one female patient even developed a crush on me. To my knowledge nobody had ever fallen in love with me before so the experience boosted my ego temporarily, until the resident psychologist assured me that this lady was clearly very much out of contact with reality.

There was, however, one aspect of my freshman psychology experience that disturbed me greatly. Many of the hospital patients talked a lot about religion. They had, it seemed, a concern for God, sin, and forgiveness. They liked to sing hymns, and on the ward piano there was a hymnal identical to the one we used in the church where I had grown up. I discovered, further, that some of the professional staff at the hospital seemed disinterested in religion, perhaps even antireligious, and it was clear to me, even as a novice, that the patients in many cases were using religion in an unhealthy way—as a neurotic crutch—just like Freud had suggested in the pages of one of my college textbooks.

My dismay became even greater when one day I mentioned to my Sunday school teacher that I was studying psychology. I respected this man highly. He had had a great influence for good in my life, but his immediate condemnation of psychology left me surprised and probably more than a little confused.

Was psychology really at odds with the Bible, I wondered? Was the church at war with the science of individual behavior? Was "General Psychology" the university course that was going to shake my faith—as some of my church friends had predicted?

At that time I had never heard of the word "integration." We never discussed religion in our psychology class; neither did psychology come up at church (except for the Sunday school teacher's reaction). I bought a book on psychology and religion, but it was so dull that I got bogged down on page two (and still have not finished it). Nevertheless, my interest in an integration of psychology and Christianity was sparked with that freshman class almost twenty-five years ago. It is an interest that persisted throughout my years in college and graduate school (especially as I read more of Freud and saw most of my Christian classmates throw over the faith during the course of their psychological training). It is an interest that has dominated much of my teaching and probably most of my writing. As a follower of Jesus Christ, a believer in the divinely inspired Word of God, and a psychologist, I want to know if psychology and the Bible are compatible. Is it possible, or even desirable, to integrate psychology and

Christianity? These are among the issues we will consider in the pages of this book.

The Possibility of Integration

It is well known that psychology and theology—at least until recently—have had a history of conflict and, at times, rivalry. Freud may not have created the rift, but his many controversial writings on the topic of religion did not do anything to heal the division. *Totem and Taboo* (1913) and *Moses and Monotheism* (1937) both dealt with the origins of religion, "explained away" many Old Testament biblical accounts, and have been criticized as being more speculative than scientific. In his most basic work on religion, *The Future of an Illusion* (1927), Freud argued that religion is an illusion, "the universal obsessional" neurosis of humanity, and a wish-fulfillment that ought to be replaced by science. Perhaps it is not surprising that this volume was greeted with a controversy that still persists, over fifty years after its publication.

Oskar Pfister, a Swiss pastor, challenged some of Freud's views in a series of letters. Jung, Adler, and other analysts joined in the debate, and during the early part of this century, some of the best-known American psychologists turned their skills to a scientific study of religious behavior. It must have been an exciting era—back in the days of Starbuck, Leuba, James, and G. Stanley Hall—when religion was an important topic for psychological investigation. But this may have threatened a lot of people, too, especially sincerely religious people like my Sunday school teacher, who were concerned lest the new psychology somehow undermine the God of Abraham, Isaac, and Jacob, or the teachings of Jesus and Paul.

After the arrival of behaviorism, the psychological study of religion waned in popularity, although some theological liberals—like William Keller, Richard Cabot, Russell Dicks, and Anton Boisen—began to see the importance of psychology for helping pastors and other church leaders to be more effective in their care of the sick, discouraged, and needy. As a result of this concern, pastoral psychology was born and it quickly developed as a discipline. But the new movement was primarily a child of the liberal churches, and the resistance to psychology among more conservative Christians persisted.

In some circles this resistance continues to the present. In an article entitled "What part hath psychology in theology?" (1975) theologian Charles Smith has argued that psychology is "intruding into theology" when it attempts to deal with life-styles, morals, or the study of religion. He wonders if even Christian psychologies are diluting the sincere "milk of the Word" and quotes Mowrer's statement that perhaps evangelical religion is in danger of selling its birthright for a mess of psychological pottage. The same concern has been echoed by Jay Adams (1970) and by a host of other Christian writers.

There is, to be sure, good basis for much of this Christian protest against psychology. Several writers (Collins, 1977; Cosgrove, 1979) have argued that modern psychology has been built on presuppositions which often are in direct conflict with the fundamental assumptions of Christianity. As a result many psychologists have reached psychological conclusions and developed counseling techniques that are in conflict with the true Word of God as revealed in the Bible. Where psychology has penetrated the church, it appears to have done so (at least until recently) through theologically liberal seminaries where beliefs in humanism, naturalism, and innate human goodness are more consistent with the assumptions of psychology as it exists today. It is not surprising that numerous evangelical Christians have written off psychology or have suggested, as does theologian Smith (1975), that in areas where psychologists speak with authority, they are really discussing theology, not psychology.

With this background we come to the first of the issues that must concern any person interested in the integration of psychology and theology. Is such integration possible? There is an inclination on my part to answer "yes" and push on, but not everyone would agree. Some might argue that the two fields are so different that they have nothing in common and hence are irreconcilable. They represent Christian and non-Christian systems which have differing and at times conflicting assumptions, views of truth, sources of authority, concepts, and language. Psychology, it might be claimed, is a science; theology is a philosophical religious system. The two fields are as unlike, it could be argued, as pharmacology and music theory.

It must be remembered, however, that psychologists and theologians both study human behavior, values, interpersonal relations, attitudes, beliefs, pathology, marriage, the family, helping, and problem areas such as loneliness, discouragement, grief and anxiety. The two disciplines have similar interests and some overlapping goals. For the study of each to proceed as if the other did not exist would be detrimental to both areas.

In addition, if we assume (as I do) that God is the source of all truth, then there will be no conflict or contradiction between truth as revealed in the Bible (studied by Bible scholars and theologians), and truth as revealed in nature (studied by scientists, including psychologists and other scholars). To use an old phrase, God's Word and God's world do not contradict—even when we are studying the truths of theology and psychology. Integration, it would seem, *is* possible even though the relating of these two fields would appear to be difficult and intellectually demanding.

I once had lunch with a systematic theologian who described psychology as being one of the few fresh areas of intellectual endeavor for Christians today. "For most evangelical scholars," my friend suggested, "their task involves refining or renewing earlier discoveries. But the Christian psychologist is like an individual standing with a machete at the edge of a jungle. There is a lot of growth to be cut away, paths to be carved out, and discoveries to be made." The integration of psychology and theology is one of our greatest challenges as psychologists and as Christians. It will not be an easy task, but I believe it can and should be attempted.

The Purpose of Integration

Even if integration is possible, one might ask Why bother? Why spend our time trying to tie together such diverse fields as psychology and theology? There are at least four responses to this question.

First, there are those who ignore the whole issue. Undoubtedly most non-Christian psychologists take this view and so, I suspect, do many Christians. There are probably many counselors who attend church on Sunday, do their psychological work during the week, and never really wrestle with the issue of how and whether their faith and their psychological work fit together.

Others openly oppose integration. Several years ago I met with a Christian professor of psychology at Cambridge. After some discussion of his research the conversation turned to my interest in integration. "Let me give you two words of advice about your work," the learned Englishman suggested. "Forget it!"

A third and related view is that integration is not needed. Jay Adams (1970) dismisses psychology as being irrelevant, harmful, and even characterized by helplessness and hopelessness. This hardly pictures a field that any theologian would want to embrace. Bill Gothard, the popular seminar leader who once dropped out of a graduate program in psychology, and Tim La Haye, the author of numerous self-help books, are among those who see no need to integrate psychology into their theological systems. Surely it is fair to state, however, that these men and many others who claim to reject psychology, nevertheless use a number of psychological terms, concepts, and techniques. In essence, they are integrating psychology and theology even while denying the need for such integration.

A fourth view is that integration is necessary and of great importance. Psychology, to a large extent, is based on humanistic-naturalistic, philosophical, and theological values, assumptions, and beliefs. In order to be objective and maximally effective the psychologist must be aware of this foundation and, as I have written elsewhere (Collins, 1977), should even consider rebuilding the discipline on a biblically based philosophical-theological foundation. Theology, in contrast, often claims to be built on biblical exegesis, but this often reflects and is based on human insight, personal experience, and cultural relativism. In order to be objective and maximally effective, the Christian theologian should have an in-depth familiarity with human behavior, the nature and influence of bias, personal influences on perception or thinking, and other findings in the social sciences.

The Bible never presents itself as a book that includes all truth about God's created beings. We learn from a study of God's written Word, but God also has permitted us to learn about his world, including mankind, through academic disciplines and sciences such as medicine, physics, and psychology. By shutting his or her eyes to psychology, the Christian is blinded to much of God's truth about mankind and often is inclined to arrive at simplistic conclusions about human behavior and counseling. Likewise, the psychologist who ignores the divine revelation as found in Scripture has a limited understanding of human beings, their place in the universe, and their possibilities for change and growth.

Several years ago, Professor Max L. Stackhouse addressed a convention of the Association of Clinical Pastoral Educators meeting in Massachusetts. He talked about the boundary between psychology and theology, described some of the turmoil within each field, noted that we often try to smuggle little bits of subject matter into and out of each other's domains, and wondered whether the boundary between psychology and theology might be growing fuzzy.

As I read this paper I wondered if we really want to break down the boundaries between psychology and theology. Assuming that it would be possible, do we really want the two fields to become one? For me, the answer is no. There must be integration, but not obliteration. Integration implies two separate but unique fields shedding light on our understanding of similar issues. Integration does not imply the disappearance of theology, the elimination of psychology, or the swallowing up of one field by the other.

Integration does, however, mean that we are living on the boundary line between two disciplines. It is easier to stay well within the borders of one's domain or field of specialty, rather than to be working on a frontier where we are not certain where the boundary is or should be, how firmly it should be maintained, or even if it should exist at all.

What, then, is the purpose of integration? First, theology and psychology together can ask questions of each other and share perspectives that can stimulate research and lead to a greater, clearer discovery and comprehension of God's truth (especially about people). Second, the task of integration keeps the channels of communications open between theologians and psychologists so that respective conclusions are used to help all of us more fully understand human beings. We can then more effectively facilitate the changes which bring individuals into spiritual and psychological wholeness. Integration occurs in a variety of

locations—clinics, hospitals, classrooms, research labora-
tories, graduate schools, and conferences. I believe,
however, that the best location for effective integration is
the theological seminary where biblical scholars and
theologians who have some interest and knowledge in
psychology can work with psychologists who are knowledgeable in theology and familiar with the Bible. If we
believe that our task involves the serious study of God's
revelation—both written and natural—then it follows that
the student of integration should seek to be a man or
woman of God who seeks the guidance of the Holy Spirit in
all of his or her integration studies and endeavors.

The Perspectives on Integration

The attempt to integrate psychology and theology is not
something new. Oskar Pfister must have been thinking
along these lines during the years when he corresponded
with Freud. Jung had an interest in the topic (1938) and so
did such psychological writers as Erich Fromm (1950),
Gordon Allport (1950), Paul Meehl (1958), O. Hobart
Mower (1961), and a host of others—including the man
who wrote that dull book that I bought during my freshman
year in college.

Today's freshman, and graduate students as well, often
expect that integration is easy, something that can be done
with one or two lectures or, at the most, in a one-semester
course. But the task is more difficult than that. Psychology
and theology are both bodies of knowledge containing a
myriad of assumptions, hypotheses, facts, approaches, and
conclusions. There is no such thing as a unified psychology
(singular) and a unified theology. Instead, there are
psychologies and theological systems (plural) which must
somehow be integrated.

At the risk of oversimplification, we might liken

integration to the problem of translation. Recently one of my books was translated from English into Chinese. The translator had some difficulty with this task, but his fluency in both languages simplified the project considerably. He was working with one Western language and one Asian language.

Suppose, however, that we wanted to translate "Western" into "Asian". Since there are many Western languages and many Asian languages, the task would become the almost impossible one of translating, for example, English, French, German, Spanish, Dutch, Flemish, Portuguese, or Swedish, into Chinese, Japanese, Tagalog, Vietnamese, Korean, or other Eastern languages.

This is our task in integration. It would be nice to think that we are concerned with the integration of a unified psychology with a clearly interpreted Bible, but it isn't that simple. Psychology is not unified, and our interpretations of the Bible differ as the result of our training, past experience, and church affiliation. Even with these obstacles, however, there have been some recent attempts to integrate psychology and evangelical-biblical theology. Let us look at a few of these.

(a) *The Denial Approach.* Paul Tournier, the Swiss counselor, is a man whom I respect deeply as a friend, intellectual giant, compassionate counselor, and humble man of God. As I wrote a book about him several years ago, he influenced me greatly and helped to clarify much of my thinking about integration.

In discussing the relationship between psychology and theology, however, Tournier has written that the tensions are more apparent than real; the result of a misunderstanding of the real issues. Theologians and therapists are not working against each other. In Tournier's opinion they are both concerned with helping troubled people, and they both use such methods as listening, comforting, and guiding. In spite of apparent evidence to the contrary,

Tournier maintains repeatedly that psychology and religion are not in conflict (Tournier, 1964, 1968). He writes that it is in God that we find the key that makes integration possible if we listen to his voice (Collins, 1973, p. 11). Apparently listening to his voice is all we need do to attain a state of integration. I greatly respect Tournier's thinking, but his assertion that no conflict exists is surely an oversimplification. There are serious differences between psychology and theology. There *is* conflict, and to deny this (pretending that integration has already occurred) neither clarifies nor solves the issue.

(b) *The Railroad Track Approach.* One of the earliest and most thought-provoking of the modern evangelical approaches to integration came in 1958 with the publication of *What, Then, Is Man? A Symposium of Theology, Psychology, and Psychiatry.* In this book a team of Lutherans headed by psychologist (and former APA president) Paul Meehl discussed a number of integration issues—issues such as faith healing, guilt, psychopathology, determinism, grace, faith, and personality. "We are prepared to state firmly," the writers of this book stated, "that he who does not come to terms with such theoretical problems as determinism, guilt, original sin, materialism, monism, conscience, and conversion cannot even begin to work out a cognitive rapprochement between Christian theology and the secular sciences of behavior" (Meehl, et. al. 1958, p. 5).

This Lutheran symposium is not easy to read, but it identified and grappled with a number of very significant integration issues. It also involved the input of theologians and Bible scholars as well as that of psychiatrists and psychologists. (That is something that does not happen very often).

What, Then, Is Man? is in some respects a classic in the field. It grapples with theological and psychological issues and makes some good attempts at integration. But even classics that identify issues are not always able to give answers. In reading this book, I get the impression that psychology and theology are like two railroad tracks— going in the same direction, linked together with common ties, but meeting each other only on the distant horizon, and then only in the mind of the beholder.

I taught a course like this once. We called it Psychology and Theology, and I taught it jointly with a competent theologian. Try as we might, there was little real integration. I would give my psychological perspective on topics like conversion or glossalalia, he would give a theological analysis, and never did the twain seem to meet.

I felt the same frustration during the spring of 1975, when roughly thirty people met at the invitation of the Christian Medical Society to discuss demon possession. After three days, I felt that the biblical scholars and the social scientists (all of whom were evangelicals) were not really communicating. We had different assumptions about epistemology and science, used different terms, and interpreted the data differently. We ended the conference enlightened and able to understand each other better, but we were no closer to real integration, even on this one topic of demonism. (For a complete transcript of this conference, see Montgomery, 1976.)

If integration is to take place, we will need the perspectives and labors of both psychologists and theologians. Such persons must have good familiarity with (and preferably some training in) the other field. They must realize that genuine integration involves more than lining up psychological terms alongside theological terms and assuming that such parallelism is integration. Moreover, they must be willing to communicate, to see issues from the other discipline's perspective, and to work openly at pulling the railroad tracks together.

(c) *The Levels of Analysis Approach.* Richard H. Bube is a Presbyterian layman, Professor of Materials Science at

Stanford, and editor of the *Journal of the American Scientific Affiliation*. In 1971 Bube published *The Human Quest*, a book with a subtitle that is more descriptive of its contents: *A New Look at Science and the Christian Faith.*[1]

There are, Bube suggested, two general theses for relating science and Christianity:

> Thesis I. The universe exists moment by moment only because of the creative and preserving power of God.
>
> Thesis II. There are many levels at which a given situation can be described. An exhaustive description on one level does not preclude meaningful descriptions on other levels.

The first thesis is clearly taught in such Bible passages as Hebrews 1:3, Colossians 1:17, and I Corinthians 8:6. If God were to "turn himself off," Bube argues, everything would cease to exist. "There is no world ruled by orderly laws except that one constantly maintained by the activity of God" (p. 28).

Thesis II is more controversial and directly relevant to the integration of psychology and Christian theology. In presenting his levels of analysis approach, Bube begins with an analysis of language. The printing on this page can be viewed from different perspectives or levels. We can look at the individual letters of the alphabet, at the phonetics, at the whole words, at the grammar, at the context, and at the ultimate content or meaning of the printed material. Each of these perspectives is more complex than the one lower, and each higher perspective embraces all of the lower levels. When my children were preschoolers they learned letters, phonetic sounds, and words on *Sesame Street*. Later, in school, they learned to spell words, to abide by the rules of good grammar, and to look for the meaning in

Figure 1

THE STRUCTURE OF THE UNIVERSE

adapted from Bube (1971)

*Level of Representation**

Ultimate	God	Theology
Human	Society	Sociology Anthropology
	Man	and Psychology
Living but nonhuman	Animals	Zoology
	Plants	Botany
Simple life	Cell	Biology
Material but nonliving	Nonliving Matter	
	Molecules	Physics and Chemistry
	Atoms	
	Elementary Particles	
Nonmaterial	Energy	Origins

Dashes mark qualitative changes.

*Concentric Representation**

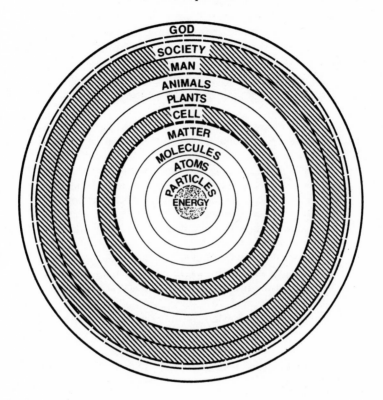

[1]From Richard Bube, *The Human Quest* (Waco, TX: Word, Inc., 1971),
by permission of the publisher.

literature. They now have moved far beyond the ABC's of *Sesame Street.*

Turning from language to the world of science, we see a more complicated, but basically similar, system of levels. This is illustrated in Figure 1. The universe may be viewed from a variety of levels, each of which can provide a valid, meaningful, but nevertheless incomplete perspective. The higher-level categories deal with questions in a more ultimate way but these levels are neither more nor less important than the lower level descriptions.

On the basis of this approach, Bube writes,

> It is no longer necessary to debate whether Christian conversion is a psychological or a theological experience. Christian conversion can be understood only when described as a psychological *and* a theological experience, as well as a biological, biochemical, and biophysical experience. It is no longer necessary to debate whether man is a machine or a person created by God. Man can be understood only when described as a machine *and* as a person created by God, created with real personality in the image of a personal God but functioning on the biological, biochemical, and biophysical levels according to the laws that govern the rest of nature as well. (1971, p. 35).

This approach acknowledges that science, because of its presuppositions and "intrinsic limitations," cannot provide answers to all our questions about the universe. But neither can theology answer all questions. Theology and science must work on similar problems, each presumably arriving at conclusions which one hopes will interlock—like the pieces of a jigsaw puzzle—to present a more complete understanding.

Such a puzzle does not fit together automatically, however. Some issues are so complex and so difficult to understand that "the best that we can do is to construct a number of different models out of our common experience, each of which will describe a different facet of reality, and all of which must be brought to bear in order to have a complete description of reality" (Bube, 1971, p. 177). Presumably this involves a variety of scientists and theologians periodically coming together (in person) to work on a synthesis of their different perspectives and conclusions.

The idea is excellent and appears to be at the basis of integration approaches proposed by Myers (1978) and Kirwan (1980). Regrettably, however, there are problems when men and women of different academic disciplines gather to work on an issue of common interest. I have already mentioned my frustration with different terminology and perspectives following the Christian Medical Society's conference on demonology—and at that meeting we were all Christians, all committed to the authority of Scripture, and apparently free of the personal competition and interdisciplinary rivalry which so often characterizes such gatherings. Several years earlier an interdisciplinary conference on the theme "What is normal?" apparently reached some of the same deadlocks (Mowrer, 1954).

The difficulties of interdisciplinary (or interlevel) communication should not cause us to reject the levels of analysis approach. It may, in time, be shown to be the most feasible procedure, and given the increasing complexity of almost all intellectual disciplines, it would seem that integration and understanding can best result from some kind of interdisciplinary approach.

(d) *The Integrated Models Approach.* John Carter and Richard Mohline, both trained in psychology and theology, took a somewhat interdisciplinary approach when they proposed their model for integration (1976). Freely admitting that their work is "like the girder structure of a skyscraper," which needs a lot of filling in before the building is completed, Carter and Mohline nevertheless proposed a creative approach based on three stated assumptions:

> (a) All truth is God's truth, therefore, the truths of psychology (general revelation) are neither contradictory nor contrary to revealed truth (special revelation) but are integrative in a harmonious whole. (b) Theology represents the distillation of God's revelation of Himself to man in a linguistic, conceptual, and cultural media man can understand and which focuses primarily on man's nature and destiny in God's program. (c) Psychology as a science is primarily concerned with the mechanisms by which man functions and the methods to assess that functioning. (Carter and Mohline, 1976, p. 4)[2]

After examining a large number of theology and psychology textbooks Carter and Mohline concluded that each of these two disciplines could be divided into the eight parallel subject areas shown in figure 2. "The nature, character, and levels of the integratable material in each area varies," the authors write (p. 6), "but we are asserting that basic principles and content of psychology are integratable into their equivalent theological area."

It is beyond the scope of our discussion to summarize how these theological and psychological sub-areas are interrelated, but as an example we might mention anthropology and personality. Anthropology, as defined theologically, is a doctrine dealing with the creation and nature of human beings. The Bible and historical Christian theology have said much about human nature, but so have contemporary psychologists. Personality theory in particular is implicitly a psychological statement about the nature of humans. "Thus . . . personality theories, however they differ in content, all make an implicit or explicit assumption about the nature of man and are therefore psychologically

Figure 2

THE SCOPE OF THEOLOGY
AND PSYCHOLOGY

adapted from Carter and Mohline (1976)

THE SCOPE OF THEOLOGY	THE SCOPE OF PSYCHOLOGY
THEOLOGY PROPER	**SCIENCE OF PSYCHOLOGY**
Angelology	Psychic Phenomena
Christology (pneumatology)	Counselor
Anthropology	Personality
Harmartiology	Psychopathology-Psychotherapy
Soteriology	Development
Ecclesiology	Social Psychology
Eschatology	Psychology of Rewards

[2]From J. D. Carter and R. J. Mohline in *Journal of Psychology and Theology, 4*, (1976), pp. 3-14. Used by permission.

equivalent to biblical anthropology" (Carter and Mohline, 1976, p. 8).

Carter and Mohline note that (a) the foci of explanation are different in theology and psychology (the former is generally historical and socio-cultural; the latter is descriptive-clinical, developmental, and experimental), (b) the levels of explanation are different (theology is metaphysical; psychology is empirical-scientific), and (c) there are different epistemologies (theology is revelational whereas psychology is scientific).

This analysis remains to be developed further, but as it has not been developed, it is easy to understand why one critic has called it a "zipper approach." It does appear that psychology has been forced into a procrustean bed of theological doctrines, and that two disciplines have been lined up and zippered together—a conclusion that is reinforced in the more recent book by Carter and Narramore (1979). Until the model is clarified further, however, it would seem to have limited usefulness, although it might be viewed as a creative application of Bube's "levels of integration" to the subject matter of psychology and theology.

(e) *The "Spoiling the Egyptians" Approach.* In a recent book on counseling, Lawrence Crabb (1977) identified three historical approaches to integration and proposed a fourth alternative.

The first approach, "separate but equal," assumes that theologians and psychologists have their own separate areas of interest and expertise. Let the theologians deal with theology, this assumes, let the psychologists study psychology, and let's keep out of each other's domain. This, Crabb concludes, is unwise, since the two disciplines deal with guilt, insecurity, self-acceptance, and a variety of other common areas of subject matter.

The "tossed salad" approach takes a little theology and a little psychology and tosses them together into various blendings, depending on the individual integrator's tastes. Crabb wonders if most Christian professionals have adopted this approach to integration: combine the insights and resources of Scripture with the wisdom of psychology and hope that a truly effective and sophisticated Christian psychotherapy will emerge (Crabb, 1977). Such an approach, however, uncritically combines the secular with the sacred in a way that could compromise each and water down the biblical position.

> The central problem with Tossed Salad integration is not that secular psychology has nothing to offer, but rather that a careless acceptance of secular ideas may lead to an unplanned compromise with biblical doctrine. Integration is not primarily a matter of aligning theology with relevant psychology. The first job of the integrationist is to screen secular concepts through the filter of Scriptures; then we can align those concepts which pass through with appropriate theological matter and attempt to assimilate them into a comprehensive whole. The Tossed Salad model fails to emphasize enough the critical and prior job of screening (1977, p. 39-40)[3]

In "nothing but-ery," the third approach (religion is "nothing but" a psychologically classifiable concept, or psychology is "nothing but" a restatement of concepts that are already in the Bible) the theologian reduces all psychology to theology or the psychologist redefines all theology in psychological terms. This ignores the contribution of the other field (or even its need for existence) and assumes that one's own field is all that is needed.

This appears to be common in psychology. Addressing members of the American Psychological Association, Allen Bergin (1977) has argued that most contemporary

---

[3]From *Effective Biblical Counseling* by Lawrence Crabb. Copyright © 1977 by The Zondervan Corporation. Used by permission.

psychological research and theory denies the sacred nature of human experience "on assumptive and methodological grounds." Because they cannot accept the existence of spiritual variables, many modern psychologists try to explain faith healing, conversion, and similar phenomena in strictly psychological terms. If this cannot be done they become like the entomologist who couldn't classify a newly found bug—so he stepped on it!

"Nothing but-ery" also appears in theology whenever it is assumed that psychology is unnecessary since it is "nothing but" that which is already recorded in the Bible. This is a viewpoint that fails to see the hand of God in nature and in science as well as in Scripture. It is a view which often leads to a smug theological superiority and a simplistic view of both human behavior and counseling.

In contrast to all this Crabb advocates an approach to integration which he calls "spoiling the Egyptians". In the book of Exodus, the Israelites took from the Egyptians what was needed for the trip through the wilderness. This "taking from" is called spoiling the Egyptians in the King James Version (Exodus 3:22).

In order to "spoil the Egyptians of secular psychology", Crabb recommends that we let Scripture be both our guide in psychology and the "infallible, inspired, inerrant revelation" against which we test our psychology. This will involve a careful weeding out of those elements in psychology that oppose the Scriptures. Such an approach is presented as an alternative better than that of the "Tossed Salad counselor who mixes concepts as they seem called for or the Nothing Butterist counselor who refuses to benefit from the insights of secular study" (p. 52).

It is interesting to read Crabb's list of qualifications for the psychologist who could work seriously in the area of integration. He or she should (a) spend at least as much time in the study of the Bible as in the study of psychology, (b) study the Bible in a regular and systematic manner, (c) have both a general grasp of the structure and overall content of Scripture as well as a working knowledge of Bible doctrine, and (d) be involved in the fellowship of a Bible-believing local church.

Not all Christian psychologists would accept these as necessary qualifications for the integrator, but perhaps many would agree that in any evangelical approach to integration, Scripture must be a standard against which we test psychology (rather than vice versa). In addition, we should be careful to avoid both "nothing but-ery" and an uncritical acceptance of psychologial concepts that may be attractive but are basically antibiblical.

Crabb is thought-provoking in his analysis, but he says relatively little about presuppositions and regrettably he gives little in the way of guidelines for "spoiling the Egyptians."

(f) *The Rebuilding Approach.* Many approaches to integration attempt to unite psychological terms and techniques with theological concepts. This appears to be characteristic of Tournier's approach, Meehl's book, and possibly the work of Carter and Mohline. If we are to really integrate psychology and theology, however, I believe we must start at a more basic level. We must start with our foundational presuppositions.

The Rebuilding of Psychology: An Integration of Psychology and Christianity (Collins, 1977) analyzes the current state of psychology and evaluates psychological (especially Freudian) criticisms of religion.[4] It notes that theologians usually are honest enough to state their fundamental beliefs and to indicate why they believe as they do. Psychologists, in contrast, often tend to assume that they can be neutral, scientifically objective, and unencumbered by underlying presuppositions. Complete neutrality, however, is a myth. We all have assumptions that influence our actions and/or conclusions, whether we

Figure 3

NEW FOUNDATION FOR PSYCHOLOGY

adapted from Collins (1977)

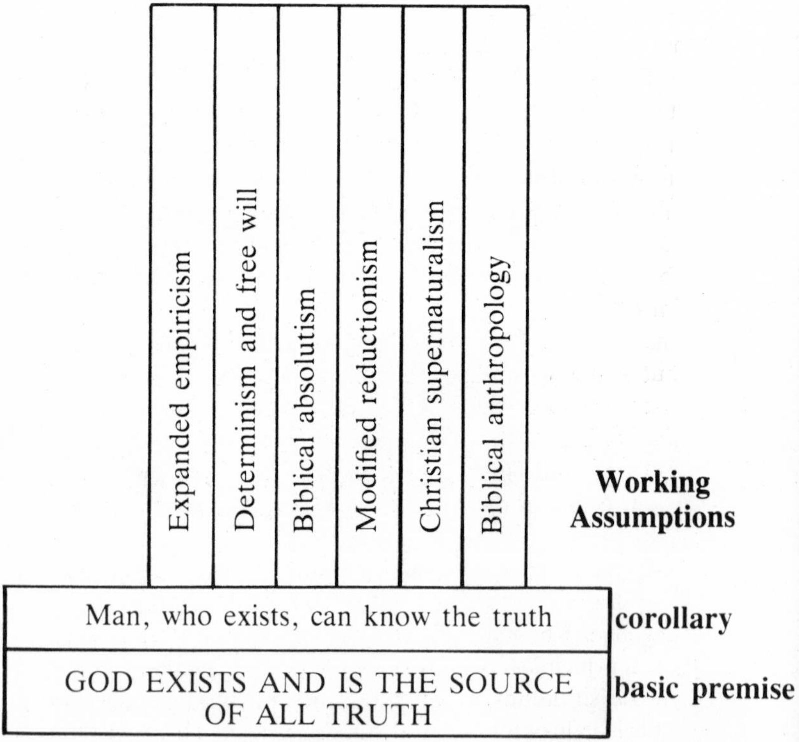

Expanded empiricism · Determinism and free will · Biblical absolutism · Modified reductionism · Christian supernaturalism · Biblical anthropology

Working Assumptions

Man, who exists, can know the truth — corollary

GOD EXISTS AND IS THE SOURCE OF ALL TRUTH — basic premise

[a]From Gary R. Collins, *The Rebuilding of Psychology: An Integration of Psychology and Christianity* (Wheaton, IL: Tyndale House Publishers, 1977), by permission of the publisher.

recognize and acknowledge such assumptions or not. Theologians realize this and write doctrinal statements; psychologists prefer to ignore the whole issue.

But we are being unscientific if we overlook so potent an influence for bias as our foundational presuppositions. Might it not be better to build our psychology on a foundation similar to that shown in Figure 3?

This model begins with the assumption that God exists and is the source of all truth. This truth is revealed through the Bible (disclosed truth) and nature (discovered truth). In our psychology work, we who are Christians accept at least six working assumptions:

—Expanded empiricism. This suggests that truth comes not only through controlled experiments, but through such sources as logical deduction, biblical revelation, and even intuition or study of the humanities. I would agree with Crabb that the Bible is our primary resource against which all other facts must be tested. But the Bible does not claim to be a textbook on psychology. We can and must draw from other nonbiblical sources if we want to understand human beings more completely and intervene to bring about maximum change through counseling.

—Determinism and free will. This, of course, is a paradox, but both alternatives appear to be taught in Scripture, and some psychologists are beginning to recognize that both must be accepted into contemporary psychology.

—Biblical absolutism. The modern mind builds moral values around some system of relativism. In contrast, the evangelical Christian searches for biblical absolutes and general principles to guide our understanding of behavior. In those situations where the Bible is silent, we try to establish values and ethical decisions as much in accordance as possible with the spirit of biblical principles.

—Modified reductionism. In our attempts to understand

human nature it is possible to break our subject matter into smaller units of analysis. Chemists have done this, so have physicists, and so too do a number of psychologists. But people are characterized by a wholeness that surely is greater than the sum of the parts. The Christian, therefore, cannot accept the widely held view that man is best studied by reducing behavior into smaller and smaller parts.

—Christian supernaturalism. This accepts the psychologist's view that the world is orderly, but it goes farther. Christian supernaturalism acknowledges that God created all things and through his Son holds everything together. This is a view which challenges and denies Fromm's assertion that "man is alone in a universe indifferent to his fate" (1947, p. 445). The Christian presupposes the existence and influence of the supernatural in human lives, and this has important implications for both understanding behavior and helping people change.

—Biblical anthropology. Unlike the humanist who presupposes human goodness and moral neutrality, the Christian assumes that we are created in God's image, are fallen creatures, and are loved by a Divine Being who has made it possible for us to return to him through faith in his Son Jesus Christ. Those who commit themselves to Jesus Christ as Savior and Lord are "born again," new creations who possess divinely given spiritual gifts and the assurance of eternal life after death.

Space does not permit us to show how such a new foundation could influence psychological research and counseling (see Collins, 1977). I believe, however, that the whole science of individual human behavior could be changed if it were to be built on such a biblically oriented base. This is integration at the foundational presuppositional level; integration that could permeate *all* of our psychological work in the future.

Figure 4

Secular and Christian Models of Psychology and Religion

adapted from Carter (1977)

SECULAR MODELS		CHRISTIAN MODELS		SUMMARY
Model	*Example*	*Model*	*Example*	
1. Psychology *against* Religion	Ellis Freud	Scripture *against* Psychology	Adams	Psychology and Religion are different. The holder of one view dismisses the other as being harmful and/or irrelevant.
2. Psychology *of* Religion	Fromm Mowrer	Scripture *of* Psychology	Relational Theology	Religion is seen as relevant to Psychology; good psychology translates the valid insights of religion into psychology and uses them for human good (or spiritual growth).
3. Psychology *parallels* Religion	Thorne	Scripture *parallels* Psychology	Clement (the two spheres are isolated) Meehl (the two spheres can be correlated)	Religion and Psychology are separate, unrelated spheres. There are parallels of interest and similar subject matter, but no interaction.
4. Psychology *integrates* Religion	Allport Frankl	Scripture *integrates* Psychology	Crabb Van Kaam Hulme Wagner Carter/Mohline	Unification of Religion and Psychology is both possible and desirable.

[5]Adapted from J.D. Carter, "Secular and Sacred Models of Psychology and Religion," *Journal of Psychology and Theology,* (5(3), 1977, p. 199. Copyright 1977. Used by permission of the Rosemead Graduate School of Professional Psychology, La Mirada, CA 90638.

Conclusion

It was E. C. Tolman, I believe, who once warned against wedding ourselves to any one theory. Surely we must hold our theories lightly, including our theories of integration. Other Christian approaches to integration are being developed, including the work of Jeeves (1976), Sall (1975), Oates (1973), Farnsworth (1974, 1976), Myers (1978), and Cosgrove (1979). Each of these illustrates the problems and the progress involved in this important and fascinating field. Carter (1977; Carter and Narramore, 1979) who has summarized much of the integration work to date, identifies four secular models of psychology and religion along with four Christian models of psychology and Scripture (see Figure 4).[5] Tentatively, Carter suggests that all approaches to the integration of faith with "the world of life and thought" can be reduced to one of these four categories.

It appears, therefore, that progress is being made in Christian approaches to integration. But how does one move from theoretical discussions, important as these are, to practical integration in the church, in counseling, and in the psychologist's daily work? It is to these issues that we turn in the next two chapters.

CHAPTER 2

Integration: The Applications I

Gary R. Collins

When I was in graduate school we used to hear a great deal about scholarship. We were encouraged to write scholarly articles, to read scholarly journals and to prepare scholarly master's theses and doctoral dissertations. Nobody gave us a definition of scholarship, and the dictionary description—"that which befits a learned and erudite person"—was not of much practical help. Perhaps many of us come to the conclusion that "scholarly" really means to be dull, boring, and irrelevant.

I would like to suggest, however, that a true scholar is someone who takes care in his or her research, striving to attain accuracy while avoiding both error and bias. The scholar is familiar with the work of other researchers or scholars in the field. In addition, the true scholar should attempt to be simple without being simplistic, able to communicate with clarity, and aware of the practical implications of his or her disciplines. One who sits isolated in an ivory tower, reading books or articles, and writing more of the same, is not my idea of a scholar.

This was an issue with which I struggled when it came time to prepare the material in these pages. The integration of psychology and theology is largely a theoretical issue. It would be easy to focus our attention on complicated technical topics, to use specialized terminology, and to keep this discussion at the dull, boring, and irrelevant level. Too often this is what happens in "scholarly" books or lectures, but I would hope for something different here. If psychology and theology can really be integrated, this integration must have practical as well as theoretical implications. It is to these practical aspects of integration that we now turn.[6]

Recently I had a brief conversation with a well-known Christian pastor and author whose seminars and books have addressed a number of psychologically related issues including marriage, sex, depression, and personality change. In our discussion this man suggested that psychology is a "godless, secular science." My friend apparently does not read psychological literature, is critical of professional counseling, and staunchly maintains that the social sciences, including psychology, have nothing to offer the local church or parachurch organizations.

As a Christian trained in psychology, I disagree. Just as truth about God's created universe may come through the natural sciences, philosophical logic, or the humanities, so can truth come by way of psychology, psychiatry, and the other social sciences. There is, of course, much within psychology that the Christian cannot accept. Some of the psychological conclusions about human nature, some of the techniques used by professional counselors, and some of the proposals for altering our future are clearly contrary to Christian ethics and the teaching of Scripture. If we test our psychological conclusions empirically, logically, and (of

[6]Portions of this and the following chapter appeared previously in "Psychology, Christian People Helping and the Church, *Journal of Christian Counseling,* Spring 1977; and in "Psychology is Not a Panacea But . . .," *Christianity Today* (November 16, 1979), by permission of the publisher. Copyright 1979 by *Christianity Today.*

prime importance) against the inspired Word of God, however, we will discover that the psychological sciences contain much that can be of practical value to the Christian who is seeking to serve Christ within the local church and without.

There are at least six major areas where Christian psychologists and their psychological conclusions can be of help to the Body of Christ. These areas are shown in Figure 5, (p. 49), which represents a wheel revolving around a central axis.

At the center is the Bible, the Word of God. This is the core around which our psychology must revolve. Without the stablizing influence of God's verbal revelation, the wheel could go spinning off uncontrolled in a variety of directions. This appears to have happened with much secular psychology, most of which rests on the shifting sands of humanism, relativism, and naturalism; views which reject the value of biblical revelation, overemphasize the importance of empiricism, and accept a deterministic self-centered view of human nature. In contrast, many Christians believe that the Scriptures are a firm core around which all psychological activities can be centered and against which we can test our psychological conclusions and techniques. The Christian interested in integration should have or develop a good understanding of Old and New Testament teaching, as well as a knowledge of hermeneutics, systematic theology, apologetics, and Christian ethics.

As stated previously, in his divine wisdom God did not choose to reveal all truth within the pages of Scripture. The Bible was never intended to be a complete psychology or counseling textbook, even though it speaks with truth and authority on psychological and counseling issues. The Christian who wants to understand and help change human behavior must have a good understanding of psychological techniques and knowledge in areas such as the biological, cognitive, affective, social, and individual bases of behavior.

The outer portion of the circle consists of six segments, three of which (on the right) refer to people, while the other three are more concerned with programs. Each of the segments deals with one specific aspect of "people-helping" as this relates to the church of Jesus Christ. In the paragraphs that follow we will comment briefly on each of the segments and then return for a discussion in more depth.

(a) *Professional People-Helping:* It is widely recognized that there is intense competition among students who want to gain admittance to graduate training programs in psychology. The number of new professionals entering the field is so large that some have begun to wonder if we are in danger of having to many psychologists. Nevertheless, it appears that a need still exists for highly qualified Christian professionals and for programs which can train such people to help individuals, couples, and families, both within the church and without.

Professional people-helpers are trained to counsel with more severely disturbed persons, but these professionals can do more. As a group they can and should be involved in training, supervising, and assisting pastoral and lay counselors; offering guidance in the establishment of church-related programs for preventing problems; helping others through the means of speaking and the writing of books or articles; mustering a defense and strong response to challenge the psychological critics of Christianity; conducting research on the effectiveness of counseling and church-related programs; contributing their expertise to the selection, training, and placement of church workers, including missionaries; and devising creative approaches for strengthening the therapeutic effectiveness of the local church and parachurch organizations.

(b) *Pastoral People-Helping:* When the government-sponsored Joint Commission on Mental Health conducted a national survey in the United States several years ago, it was discovered that almost half of all persons in need of counseling had sought help from a clergyman (Joint Commission, 1961). Some of the reasons for this are not difficult to discover. Pastors are more accessible than professional counselors, more numerous, and much less costly. Furthermore, the pastoral counselor has less of a stigma attached to his or her position. It is much less threatening to conclude, "I'll talk with my minister (or priest) about a problem," than to think, "I'm so far gone that I need a psychiatrist." Church leaders also bring the healing balm of religion, and because they are more familiar figures they are more often trusted than the professional, who still is seen by many as an aloof "mind reader" or "head shrinker."

In addition to its research, the Joint Commission made some startling conclusions about pastoral people-helping. "Pastoral counseling by clergymen is unquestionably the single most important activity of the churches in the mental health field," the Commission report stated.

A host of persons untrained or partially trained in mental health principles and practices—clergymen . . . and others—are already trying to help and to treat the mentally ill in the absence of professional resources. . . .With a moderate amount of training through short courses and consultation on the job, such persons can be fully equipped with an additional skill as mental health counselors. . . . Teaching aid must be provided to . . . schools of theology . . . and others so that they may have part-time or full-time faculty members who will integrate mental health information into the training programs of these professions." (1961, pp. 134, 257)

Since the appearance of these words, seminaries and other training institutions have spent considerable effort, time, and money in programs designed to train pastors and potential pastors as people-helpers. The training has just begun and in the future should be more in-depth, more practical, and more integral a part of the seminary curricula. On the other hand, many pastors are functioning at full capacity whether trained in counseling or not. Many pastors are swamped with counselees, overwhelmed by the needs all around, frustrated by a lack of time for their non-counseling work, and unable to find professionals to whom needy people can be referred. More and more it is becoming clear that lay people within the church must be trained as people-helpers and encouraged to rejoice with those who rejoice, weep with those who weep, and bear one another's burdens (Rom. 12:15; Gal. 6:2).

(c) *Peer People-Helping:* When people have a personal problem, to whom do they first turn for help? Many might go to a friend, neighbor, or relative. These are the people who understand us best and who are most readily available in times of need. They comprise what is perhaps the most influential people-helping force in the country.

Friends and relatives of needy people can be very effective as people-helpers. When Robert Carkhuff (1968) surveyed the literature on peer or "paraprofessional" helpers, he concluded that laypersons, with or without training, could counsel as well as, and in some cases better than, professional counselors. This was true whether the peer counselors were working with normal adults who were having problems, with children, with psychiatric patients in out-patient clinics, or with psychotics in psychiatric hospitals. Unconcerned about professionalism and more relaxed, informal, down to earth and compassionate, these lay counselors have demonstrated that they can be highly competent people-helpers.

(d) *Psychological-Apologetic People-Helping:* Several decades ago, when the evolution controversy was a frequent topic of discussion among Christians, biology was the greatest intellectual threat to the church. Within recent years, however, psychology has taken over this role. It is well known that Freud attacked religion in many of his writings, and generations of psychologists have been critical ever since.

The Christian student entering a university classroom often hears convincing arguments designed to prove, among other conclusions, that conversion is primarily an emotional reaction to persuasion techniques, that prayer is wishful thinking, that miracles were and are impossible and not to be believed in this nonscientific era, that ritual (including worship) is evidence of compulsive and obsessive neuroses, that God is a projection of our imagination or an illusory father figure, or that all religion is a result of conditioning. If the student has not been prepared to counteract such teaching, he or she sometimes can be persuaded to abandon the faith in response to the conclusions of psychological science, which, in some respects, is a religion in itself (see Vitz, 1977).

Most, if not all, of these psychological arguments, can be answered decisively by Christian apologetics—that field of study concerned with defending the truthfulness of the Christian religion. Freshman students in psychology classes do not often realize this, however, and neither do many of their professors. As psychology becomes more technical and sophisticated, so can its arguments against religion, especially Christianity. Scholars who are committed and knowledgeable Christians, familiar with the Scriptures, able to think clearly, and thoroughly acquainted with the methods and conclusions of modern psychology, must set themselves to the task of clearly answering and decisively counteracting these psychological challenges to the Christian faith. This is a new and crucial role, especially for the professional people-helper.

(e) *Public People-Helping:* When somebody writes a book about human needs, prepares an article, or gives a speech, it is easy for him or her to be misinterpreted. All of us, but needy people especially, hear or see only what we are looking for, and we sometimes pull phrases out of context in an attempt to find help with a problem.

In spite of these dangers, it appears that thousands of people look to the media for help, and many apparently find solace and guidance by reading or listening to tapes, sermons, and how-to lectures. Professional psychologists are inclined to criticize such public people-helping, especially when naive people are led to believe that a book or self-help formula can solve all problems quickly and permanently. Human difficulties are rarely that simple, and when a formula is tried and does not work, the user often feels guilty for the failure, especially if the formula for help is tied to the Bible and presented as the Scriptural answer to the user's problems.

It must be remembered, however, that this is the only help that some people will get. Since it can be threatening and uncomfortable to talk about problems, even to one's friends, many people turn to books, tapes, or lectures, hoping that these will provide help in a more anonymous way. And undoubtedly such help *is* provided!

Surely, however, public people-helping could be better—clearer, more realistic in its promises, more biblically based, more alert to the established findings of modern psychology, and less dependent for support on single case histories, on the personal experiences of the communicator, or on poor biblical exegesis. Public people-helping, to be truly effective, must also be based on the clearly established principles of homiletics and communication. It must give more emphasis to individual differences so that people can feel less guilty if the principles or suggestions fail to work in their own lives. And the public people-helper should emphasize the value and respectability of discussing one's problems with a friend, pastor or professional counselor—instead of seeking all one's help in the impersonal pages of a book or the generalized words of a sermon outline.

(f) *Preventive People-Helping:* It is an established conclusion within the medical profession that prevention is the best way to counteract disease. Vaccination programs, health education, and community programs for disease control are some of the more familiar ways in which illness is avoided and prevented from spreading.

Thus far, the main thrust of preventive psychology programs has been an attempt to change communities by eliminating poverty, crime, and other stressful influences that affect our psychological well-being. This, however, is not the only approach to prevention and perhaps is not even the best approach.

We must help people identify and avoid potential stresses in their own lives and marriages. (Premarital counseling, for example, does this.) We must help people to anticipate and prepare for future crises such as retirement, divorce, or death. We must help lay people to spot developing problems in others so that help can be made available before a problem gets worse. We must learn how worship, study programs, discussion groups, church socials, and other activities—religious and otherwise—can help people avoid or cope more effectively with the developing problems of life.

With the possible exception of the school, there is no institution in the community more strategic than the chuch for preventing psychological problems. The church is in contact with whole famlies over extended periods of time. Church leaders can visit in homes and are present both in times of crisis and at the turning points of life (such as marriage, retirement, or death). Sunday school teachers, youth leaders, elders, deacons, and other lay persons within the Body of Christ work closely with fellow Christians and are able to intervene in helpful non-threatening ways before serious problems develop.

Psychology, especially preventive and community psychology, can and must help the church in this crucial problem of prevention. It is still a new field and holds considerable promise, especially if the principles of prevention are built on, and are consistent with, the teachings of Scripture.

The six segments of Figure 5 clearly relate to the ministry of the local church. The integration of psychology and theology already has shown itself to be a practical possibility in each of these area. Nevertheless, the influence of professional, pastoral, peer, psychological-apologetic, public, and preventive psychology is not limited to the local body of believers.

Consider, for example, how this circle could apply to missions. *Professional* psychologists possess expertise which could be used in selecting, training, and counseling missionaries and their families. Most basic counseling principles are universal, and *pastoral* counseling and psychology can be beneficial, both to pastors as they minister to their own people, and to missionaries as they help new Christians, themselves, and each other. *Peer* people-helping also occurs in other cultures, although the concept of psychological training for laity appears at present to be less accepted and developed abroad than in English-speaking North America. With the spread of psychology to other cultures, the psychological criticism of Christianity (and Christian missions) seems almost sure to increase. *Psychological-apologetics,* therefore, could be helpful preparation for missionaries and national Christian leaders alike. *Public* people-helping is very important to missions—perhaps even more important in societies where open discussion of personal problems is culturally discouraged. Problems do develop in people everywhere, however, and pastors at home and abroad can benefit from some knowledge of the *prevention* of difficulties.

We can also go around the circle in a consideration of marriage and the family—surely one of the most pressing areas of interest in our modern society. *Professionals*

Figure 5

PSYCHOLOGY AND THEOLOGY: AREAS OF PRACTICAL INTEGRATION

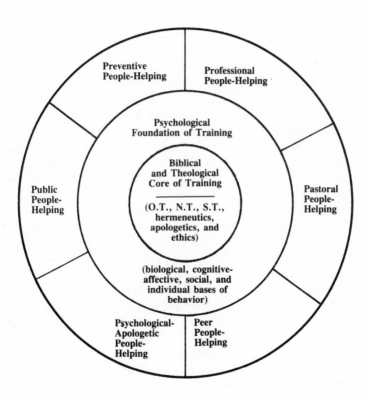

clearly have a significant role in marriage and family counseling; so do *pastoral* counselors. H. Norman Wright of Biola College has shown in his Marriage Enrichment Seminars that couples can be trained to help other couples with marriage problems. This is only one of several *peer* people-helping programs for families. With the emphasis (often psychologically based) on non-Christian alternative styles of marriage, there is a need for a solid apologetic in support of biblically based ways of relating in the home. *Public* people-helping in the area of marriage, family, and single life has become the topic of numerous books and several seminars. Christian psychologists may despair at some of the advice given in these public programs, but rather than despair, we have an obligation to do a better job than is currently being done. Then, of course, there is a need for more attention to ways in which marriage- and family-related problems can be *prevented.*

Seminaries and Christian colleges, youth programs, evangelistic associations, radio and television broadcasting—these and other church-related organizations could all benefit from the six facets of a biblically based psychology. In years gone by, we have trained a few Christian professionals and focused attention on training pastors to counsel with their parishioners in times of crisis. It is now time to broaden our concept of psychology and its role in the church of Jesus Christ. Psychology is not a panacea—the answer to all our problems. But this science of human behavior does have practical value for the Christian, value that is much greater than most believers have recognized. A challenge now exists for Christian professionals and non-psychologists to work together in an effort to build a biblically based psychology which can have a much broader influence on the lives of Christians, local churches, and parachurch organizations. This is a major goal of integration.

Having considered this broad outline, let us now look in

more detail at the six integration areas. We will start with professional applied psychology.

Professional People-Helping

At a recent psychology convention one of the speakers commented that as yet there is no such thing as a Christian theory of counseling. Certainly there are no highly developed Christian approaches to counseling, but a variety of theoretical approaches currently are being developed. Crane (1970), Drakeford (1961, 1967), Morris (1974), Clyde Narramore (1960), Roberts (1950), Smith (1976), Stapleton (1976), and Collins (1972, 1976a, 1980a) are among those professionals and nonprofessionals who have written about counseling from a Christian perspective. Koch (1965) has focused on occultism and Christian counseling, while Crabb (1975, 1977) and Solomon (1977) have each proposed approaches that are unique in their biblical perspective. Perhaps the best known of the Christian systems is the nouthetic counseling of Adams (1970, 1973), although this might more accurately be listed as a pastoral, rather than a professional, approach. To this list we could add the work of Catholic writers such as Kennedy (1977) and Egan (1975), although these are not particularly religious in their emphasis. Then, there is the whole perspective of the more liberal Protestant writers (mostly pastoral counselors) such as Hiltner (1958) or Clinebell (1965). These and a number of other Christian approaches have been summarized in a recent book (Collins, 1980b).

Are these and similar approaches in any way unique because they are proposed by people who claim to be Christians and want to make their Christianity a part of counseling? To answer this question, we must consider the assumptions, the goals, and the techniques of counseling.

Assumptions. As recent writers have recognized (Collins, 1977; Cosgrove, 1979), psychology today, including counseling–clinical psychology, is built on a set of assumptions that for the most part acknowledge the importance of empiricism, determinism, relativism, reductionism, and naturalism. In contrast, many Christians would agree that knowledge can come from a variety of sources, including the Bible; that we have free will, even though much of our behavior is determined; that there are moral absolutes; and that a personal God exists who reveals himself, intervenes in the affairs of people, and holds the whole universe together by his power.

All of this has relevance for counseling because, to a large extent, our perceptions, therapeutic goals, and helping techniques are determined by our presuppositions. For example, both the Christian and the nonbeliever would agree that personal problems can arise from some combination of physical disease, psychological pressures, and social-environmental influences. The Christian, however, because of his or her assumptions that a personal God exists and that we can find truth in divine revelation (a) can also see the possibility of supernatural forces acting in a life and (b) can recognize the harmful effects of sin.

Goals. With these somewhat different perspectives on the causes of abnormality, there also may be a difference in goals. Of course, Christians and non-Christians alike would agree on such therapeutic purposes as changing the counselee's behavior or attitudes, teaching social or academic skills, encouraging the expression of emotions, giving support in times of crisis, clarifying values, teaching responsibility, instilling insight, or guiding in the making of decisions. The Christian, however, also may be concerned about stimulating spiritual growth, helping counselees to experience forgiveness, teaching biblical truths, encouraging the confession of sin, and helping believers to grow as disciples of Jesus Christ. To reach these goals, there may be a variation in counseling techniques.

Techniques. Certainly the Christian people-helper uses many of the same methods that are part of the secular counselor's repertoire. Listening, encouraging, clarifying, confronting—these are among the techniques of every good counselor. But the Christian discourages the counselee from engaging in behavior that contradicts the Scriptures. In addition, the Christian counselor also may refer to the Bible during the interview, may choose to pray with the counselee, or may openly discuss God and spiritual matters as an integral part of the therapy.

When Adams first attacked the counseling profession several years ago (1970), many of us reacted with resistance, defensiveness, and (let us be honest) anger. It was not pleasant to be accused of having sold out our Christianity to psychology, or of having sprinkled "secular anthropological views of counseling" with a few Scripture verses in an attempt to make what we were doing look Christian. Although few of us agreed that Adams' confrontational approach was *the* biblical way to counsel, I suspect many of us could see some truth in Adams' critique of the profession. I, for one, rethought my approach and proposed an orientation that I hoped would be more biblical, and less reactionary, than nouthetic counseling (Collins, 1976).

The Christian professional faces some unique challenges today. He or she can give technical guidance to people working in the other five areas of the integration circle: pastoral, peer, psychological-apologetic, public, and preventive people-helping. The Christian also has the challenge of developing uniquely Christian approaches to counseling and showing that such approaches are effective.

In all this theory building, however, we must be flexible. It is easy to equate Christian counseling with biblical counseling and then proceed to assume that ours is "true" biblical counseling which cannot change or grow. In doing so we forget that counseling is a growing, developing field, and conclude that our own exegesis is perfect. Since each of us is a fallible human being, we must be open to new findings in counseling methodology, to new understandings of the Scripture, and to the new Christian counseling approaches that will appear in the future.

The road ahead is long, but the path to Christian counseling and professional people-helping is both exciting and filled with possibilities.

Pastoral People-Helping

When I was first invited to teach pastoral counseling in a seminary, my reaction (to say the least) was less than enthusiastic. Many of my graduate school classmates had gone on to secular universities, and I could see no prestige or future potential as a teacher in a place that had four names—Trinity, Evangelical, Divinity, and School—each of which was bad from the perspective of a psychologist.

It did not take long for me to realize, however, that the seminary could be an important place for anyone interested in integration and in teaching people how to counsel. If we can believe that more people take their problems to religious leaders than to any other professional group, then it is crucial that these leaders have the highest quality training possible. They get this training primarily in a seminary or Bible college. It is there, surrounded by biblical and theological experts, that counselor training along with theoretical integration should take place.[7]

---

[7]Portions of this section of the chapter originally appeared in Gary R. Collins, "The Pulpit and the Couch," *Christianity Today* (August 29, 1975), by permission of the publisher. Copyright 1975 by *Christianity Today*.

The pastoral psychology movement was begun by some pastors and physicians about fifty years ago. Beginning with the work of Anton T. Boisen, a minister and writer who was concerned with the need to train seminary students for work with the mentally ill, "Clinical Pastoral Education" (CPE) has grown to become a highly organized movement which provides supervised counseling training for seminarians and pastoral counselors. In many respects CPE work has been admirable: providing standards and guidelines for training pastoral counselors, alerting hospital personnel to the relevance and importance of pastoral involvement in treating the physically and mentally ill, investigating ways in which theology and psychology can be related, demonstrating the importance of counseling training to seminary education, and training seminarians in personal and spiritual development so that they are better able to counsel effectively.

From its beginning, CPE was a theologically liberal movement, and this, coupled with a general distrust of psychology, undoubtedly caused evangelicals and theologically conservative seminaries to stay apart from the CPE mainstream. Now, of course, most conservative seminaries and Bible schools have courses in pastoral counseling and some of these institutions even have highly developed departments of pastoral psychology and counseling. Nevertheless, evangelical contact with the CPE movement has tended to remain minimal.

It must be recognized, of course, that pastoral counselors, like theologians, cover a broad theological spectrum. Some of the most familiar names in the mainstream movement—William Hulme, Wayne Oates, Carroll Wise, and John Sutherland Bonnell, for example—take a more sympathetic view of conservative theology than men like Seward Hiltner, Ernest Bruder, Edward Thornton, Russell Dicks, or, perhaps, Howard Clinebell.

Where does this leave those of us who are evangelical in

our theology and sensitive to the counseling ministry of the church? Are we left with Jay Adams (1970) as our only effective spokesman for a biblically based approach to pastoral counseling?

The Old Testament is filled with examples of godly men and women who were used by the Holy Spirit to encourage, guide, support, confront, advise, and in other ways help those in need. Jesus was described as a "Wonderful Counselor," and his followers were appointed, not only to preach, but to deal with the spiritual and psychological needs of individuals (Matt. 10:7, 8). Later, the New Testament Epistles gave great insight into the counseling techniques of their inspired writers. Throughout the Christian era, church leaders have engaged in what have been called the four pastoral functions: healing, sustaining, guiding, and reconciling.

In view of this historical background, Oates surely is correct in his statement that the church leader today does not have the privilege of deciding whether or not to counsel people. They will continue to come with their needs and hurts. The pastor's choice is not "between counseling or not counseling, but between counseling in a disciplined and skilled way and counseling in an undisciplined and unskilled way" (Oates, 1959, p. vi). Before us there is a challenge to show pastors how to counsel in a skilled way, and a way that is clearly based on the teachings of Scripture.

Pastoral psychology has largely been ignored by psychologists and scorned by Christian professional counselors. For many it is a low prestige appendage to the counseling profession. In professional circles, as well as in our churches, seminaries, and Christian colleges, we need an attitude of cooperation, mutual encouragement, and openness to psychological education so that integration can take place in one of our most needy areas—the local church.

Paraprofessional People-Helping

It has been said that the local church is not so much a showcase of saints as it is a shelter for sinners. None of us is perfect, and in spite of some churches which try to display the contrary, we Christians are struggling people who need each other for encouragement, support, stimulation, and help. The New Testament repeatedly emphasizes the importance of believers' doing things with and for one another. "Love one another," "outdo one another in showing honor," we read (Rom. 12:10), "Live in . . . harmony with one another" (15:5), "welcome one another" (15:7), "instruct one another" (15:14), "greet one another" (16:16), "through love, be servants of one another" (Gal. 5:13), "bear one another's burdens" (6:2), "forbearing one another" (Eph. 4:2), "be subject to one another" (5:21), "encourage one another" (I Thess. 5:11). Clearly, members of the Body of Christ are to be concerned about doing good to all people, but especially to those who are fellow believers (Gal. 6:10).

These scriptural instructions surely are consistent with the new and developing interest in paraprofessional counseling. Carkhuff (1967) jolted the counseling profession many years ago when he demonstrated that, in general, the patients of lay counselors do as well as, or better than, the patients of professional counselors. Many years ago, we in the church came to recognize that lay men and women could teach. More recently we have begun to see that evangelism is the responsibility of every believer—not just the job of the pastor or itinerant crusade leader. Now the time has come for us to make the same shift in counseling. Lay people can, should, and must become people-helpers. To assist them in doing so is a major challenge for contemporary psychology, and another key area for integration of psychology and theology.

Several programs have appeared for the training of peer counselors (Carkhuff, 1969; Danish, 1973; Egan, 1975;

Kagan, 1975), and more recently programs have been developed for the specific task of training lay counselors within the church. Lindquist (1976) and Wright (1977) have each written books on lay counseling, and Wright (1976) is among those who have produced training tapes. Initial research with one program (Collins, 1976*a, b*) has demonstrated that Christian peer counselors can raise their levels of empathy, warmth, and genuineness, and increase counseling skills as the result of a relatively brief training program. The further training of lay persons should take place within the local church and church-related organizations. Such training must focus on issues such as the selection of lay helpers for training, the teaching of counseling skills and techniques, the development of counselor attributes, the methods of crisis intervention, the identification of potential and developing problems in oneself and others, the importance and the techniques of referral, the evaluation of self-help formulae or books, the ways of building greater family unity and stability, and some understanding of the dynamics and treatment of depression, anxiety reactions, self-esteem problems and other common adjustment difficulties.

Does this have anything to do with integration? I believe it does. Judging from the number of popular books and articles on psychology, it would appear that lay people have a keen interest in the subject. But there is a tendency in all of us, I suspect, to believe anything that appears in print or is stated by some "expert." We must help lay people to be more astute in their evaluation of psychological insights and to see how the Bible and psychology can both be relevant to helping people with their problems.

Conclusion

The integration of psychology and theology is not some ivory tower theoretical issue, lacking relevance for individuals in the church and society. Integration involves people—professionals, pastors or other church leaders, and paraprofessionals. Integration must be a team effort involving not only professional expertise, but also drawing on the insights and involvement of persons untrained in psychology, psychiatry, or related disciplines. Integration must involve not only psychologists who have an in-depth understanding of theology and the Bible; it must involve theologians and biblical scholars who can see the benefits of God's natural revelation as revealed in psychology, who are not threatened by psychology, who have an interest in and an understanding of the field, and who are willing to work at making integration biblical, psychologically sound, and practical. Three very practical areas for integration are prevention, public people-helping, and what we are calling psychological apologetics. These are the other three parts of our circle to which we turn in the next chapter.

CHAPTER 3

Integration: The Applications II

Gary R. Collins

In my field of study, it is possible to approach one's subject matter from two perspectives. The *broad-expansive* approach, which looks at the field widely, is aware of its historical background and its current developments and future potential. In contrast, the *in-depth* approach looks at specific issues within a field and analyzes them in great detail. While I have no research data to support my observation, I suspect that people who take a broad-expansive approach tend to be visionary, creative individuals who are impatient with details. The in-depth people, on the other hand, strive to do things precisely, are alert to details and often disinterested in nonspecific generalities.

If we are to make advances in the integration of psychology and theology, we will need visionary thinkers who can synthesize broad concepts, as well as those who are astute, precision-oriented detail men or women. Consider, for example, the professional people-helping that we discussed previously. There is a need for those who can look at the whole field, evaluate what is happening, and identify similarities, differences, dangers, and trends. But we also need people who can rigorously critique and empirically study specific theories, techniques, and counseling assumptions. Perhaps this two-perspective approach is even more necessary when we come to the fourth segment of our integration-wheel: psychological apologetic people-helping.

Psychological Apologetic People-Helping

Edward John Carnell, a giant figure in the history and development of Christian apologetics, defined apologetics as "that branch of Christian theology which answers the question, Is Christianity rationally defensible?" (1948, p. 7). Apologists, Carnell suggested, have been commissioned by the church to answer (and help students answer) the critical objections that are raised against "either Christ, salvation, or the truth of the Bible." The purpose of apologetics is twofold: to bring glory to God and to leave the critics no excuse for not repenting before God. Carnell implied one other purpose—to strengthen Christians whose beliefs and moral standards are so often attacked by skeptical and critical nonbelievers.

Historically, these attacks have come from a variety of disciplines—philosophy, biology, and natural science, to name the most obvious. Within recent years, however, the battleground appears to have shifted to the social sciences. A Christian friend of mine, a biologist and chairman of the science division in a large state university on the West Coast, recently reflected this view in a casual comment. "If I were starting over," he stated, "I'd not go into biology. I'd enter the field of psychology because that's where the real battle is taking place between science and Christianity." A similar view was expressed by psychologist Mary Stewart Van Leeuwen who titled a recent paper "The View from the Lion's Den: Integrating Psychology and Christianity in the Secular University Classroom" (1977).

There are a number of areas where psychology opposes Christianity—areas of opposition that might well be answered with what might be termed "psychological apologetics." These are areas of study where theologians, apologists, and psychologists must pool their skills and observations, and the broad expansive approach must be combined with in-depth analysis. At the risk of oversimplification (and of leaving out something important), I would like to suggest that there are at least three major issues to be dealt with by psychological apologetics: the influence of models, the place of the Bible in psychology, and the problem of religious experience.

The Influence of Models. In order to help us understand complicated subject matter, both science and religion rely on analogies or models. A model is a picture, or small copy, of something that is too complicated to grasp directly. When the scientist works with a model, he or she is trying to simplify things by showing how a problem or object is "like something" with which we are familiar. A blueprint, for example, is a model of a larger building, a diagram of a football play is a model of the action on the field, and a mathematical formula could be a model of what happens when a chemical reaction occurs. In every case a model is only a partial picture of reality. In constructing models we try to select the important elements of the problem or object, and overlook everything else.

The Bible uses models (more often called analogies) to communicate ideas about spiritual reality. For example, to describe the relationship between man and God in terms of sheep and the shepherd, the branches and the vine, or the chickens and the hen, is to use models which help us understand more clearly.

Psychology also uses models to clarify understanding. Just as both a road map and a relief map give useful but somewhat limited pictures of a geographical area, so each of the psychological models gives a useful but limited perspective on human beings. Behaviorism is one model or way of looking at behavior, but it is not the only model, nor is it necessarily the best. The same could be said for psychoanalysis, humanism, existentialism, and every other psychological approach. All models of human behavior are built on several unverifiable faith-assumptions, and no single model can account for all human behavior and experience.

What does all of this have to do with integration? According to Van Leeuwen, most secular theorists assume that their model is the only accurate picture of reality and instruct their students accordingly. But . . .

> once a student realizes that every "model of man"—be it behaviorist, psychodynamic, humanistic, or whatever—proceeds on certain faith-assumptions and certain types of evidence to the exclusion of others, he has come a long way toward breaking the seductive intellectual bondage in which that model will otherwise hold him. If a teacher constantly reiterates that the various theories and techniques of psychology are not breakthroughs to essential reality, but rather approximations to reality (and even then only to a particular slice of it)—then I can say with confidence that that teacher has engaged in a very strategic piece of "pre-evangelism," to use Schaeffer's terms, without even having mentioned the name of Jesus Christ. Why? Because the student who realizes that every model of man is both incomplete and based on inescapable faith-assumptions is that much closer to accepting the possibility that there can be a revealed truth, also accepted on faith and also not exhaustive in its description of reality, which is nevertheless an essential ingredient in the understanding of man's behavior . . . The teaching of psychology after a "models of man" strategy has the effect of breaking up such limited mental sets and leaving the non-Christian student open to seeing the possibility, if not the necessity of the Christian model of man being just as worthy of consideration as any other, and certainly no

more prone to the accusation of having untestable
faith-assumptions. (1976).[8]

Much of the academic conflict between psychology and
Christian theology comes from the debate over which
model of man is "right." Students read books like *The
Future of an Illusion* (Freud, 1927), *Science and Human
Behavior* (Skinner, 1953), *Beyond Freedom and Dignity*
(Skinner, 1971), or even *Walden Two* (Skinner, 1948), and
conclude that a Christian model of man is untenable. Such
faulty thinking needs to be challenged, perhaps along the
lines that Van Leeuwen suggests. This must be a part of
psychological apologetics.

The Place of the Bible in Psychology. Several years ago,
Harold Lindsell published a very controversial book
entitled *The Battle for the Bible* (1976). He argued that
biblical inerrancy is the most important theological topic of
this age, and started the book by stating his basic premise
that "the only true and dependable source of Christianty
lies in the book we call the Bible." Lindsell's volume was
greeted with acclaim, rebuttals, and debates, all of which
indicated that the term "battle" was an appropriate title for
the book.

As a psychologist, I lack both the technical expertise and
the inclination to enter what appears to have become, at
least in some circles, a hostile, mudslinging war. I do
believe, however, that as Christian psychologists we must
give clear thought to questions of epistemology, authority,
and the authenticity of biblical revelation. This gets us into
apologetics. Psychology attacks Christianity on issues such
as these, and some Christians, in turn, have ridden on these
issues in their attacks on psychology.

---

[8]From M.S. Van Leeuwen, "The view from the lion's den: Integrating
psychology and Christianity in the secular university classroom,"
Christian Scholar's Review, 5 (1976) by permission of the publisher.

At the crux of the debate (at last for psychology), is the question of whether the Bible is the ultimate authority against which psychology must be tested, or whether psychological insights and conclusions take precedence so that the teaching of Scripture is reinterpreted by current cultural mores or psychological understanding.

In a paper presented to the Evangelical Theological Society, McQuilken (1975) creatively addressed this issue. He identified five levels of subject matter (as shown in Figure 6) and proposed that the higher the level, the greater the "functional control" of Scripture over the disciplines.

You will notice that psychology is at the second highest level. Its subject matter—the nature of humans and their relationships—so extensively overlaps with the subject matter of Scripture, that the Bible must be allowed to exercise great control over psychology. Since Scripture does not claim to be a textbook of psychology, the understanding of human nature and behavior may be "extended by empirical research and experimentation." Nevertheless, the control of Scripture over psychology (especially human psychology—as opposed to animal psychology) must be great. According to this view, it is not surprising to find that in the higher levels of this continuum, where there is maximum overlap between the Scripture and the subject matter of an academic discipline, there is also maximum potential for conflict.

, McQuilkin (1975) argues his case clearly and effectively.

> What does "under the authority of Scripture" mean for the behavioral scientist? It means that all the basic data about the nature of man, the way he should relate to other men, to his Creator and to the creation must be derived from Scripture. Areas to which Scripture does not speak may legitimately be investigated, tentative theories postulated and put to use. However, both methods and conclusions must bow to revealed truth whenever there is

Figure 6

Levels of Functional Control

adapted from McQuilkin (1975)

Level of Functional Control	Description	Example
I (highest)	Subject matter completely overlaps with revelation so that control will mean the ideas should be derived from Scripture exclusively	theology, Christian philosophy
II	Overlap with revelation is great, though not complete so that subject matter should be derived from Scripture but extended by empirical research and experimentation.	psychology, sociology, anthropology
III	Overlap with revelation is slight so that subject matter should be derived from natural sources but remain under the judgment of Scripture for its interpretation and application.	history, the arts
IV	No direct overlap with revelation so that subject matter may be derived wholly from natural sources but should be compatible with Scriptural truth.	physical science
V (lowest)	Subject matter may be unrelated to Scripture.	typing or other manual skills

[9]From J.R. McQuilken, "The behavioral sciences under the authority of Scripture." Paper presented at the Evangelical Theological Society, Jackson, MS, December 30, 1975. Used by permission.

conflict. But if the hermeneutics of Scripture, the basis of interpreting Scripture, is from the perspective of cultural anthropology or naturalistic psychology, for example, Scripture is no longer the final authority. Cultural relativism, environmental determinism and other antibiblical concepts will seep in and gradually take control. . . . In the next two decades the greatest threat to biblical authority is the behavioral scientist who would in all good conscience man the barricades to defend the front door against any theologian who would attack the inspiration and authority of Scripture while all the while himself smuggling the content of Scripture out the back door through cultural or psychological interpretation.

This, of course, is already happening. At a widely reported meeting of the Christian Association for Psychological Studies (CAPS), I chaired a panel discussion on demonology. One of the speakers, a psychologist and professed evangelical, expressed his doubts about the literal existence of an unseen demonic realm, suggesting instead that empirical scientific investigation and findings should determine our conclusions about demons, rather than the "assumptions that were current in Bible times." This conclusion led to heated debate which lasted far into the night. It is a debate that continues and must be faced in any discussion of psychological apologetics or of the broader issue of integration: Are the Scriptures really authoritative, even over psychology? Once again, McQuilkin (1975) states the issue incisively.

We are in great danger of the wide-scale subversion of biblical authority by those who are committed to that authority on the conscious and theoretical level, but who through uncritical use of behavioral scientific methodology have unwittingly come under its control.

The functional control of Scripture over any discipline must be achieved through the integration of biblical and extra-biblical ideas in one person's mind.

A committee of scientists and theologians can never do this integration. To house the anthropology department next door to the Bible department won't do it either. Functional authority of one idea over another can take place only in one's mind. To have a school of psychology next to a school of theology does not mean the Bible will actually control the work of the psychologists. The theologians may theorize with amateurish ideas about psychology and the psychologists select theological input on the basis of their own expertise in psychology. Even though working closely with Bible scholars—indeed perhaps because working together—the behavioral scientists will tend to use scripture texts to tack a Bible-colored veneer over stuff built wholly from the categories of naturalistic empiricism. Continuing interaction between theologians and behavioral scientists is very desirable and will result in good things for God's people. But my contention is that true integration, as distinct from helpful interaction, must be accomplished by individuals with dual competence.[9]

The evangelical psychological-apologist must be committed to the proposition that Scripture is authoritative over psychology. He or she must also be knowledgeable in psychology, theology, and apologetics. That is a requirement that regrettably few people are able to meet.

The Problem of Religious Experience. When the secular psychologist criticizes Christianity, the challenge often begins with the issue of religious experience. Freud, of course, reinterpreted religious experience psychologically (1927, 1928) and so have a number of others, including Fromm (1950, 1966), Frankl (1975), and a controversial British psychiatrist named William Sargant (1957, 1975).

The arguments of these and similar writers can be very persuasive. There *is* truth in many of their observations, and the psychologically or apologetically naive reader can easily be swayed to reach the conclusion that religion is nothing but a figment of the imagination, put forth for the purpose of allaying fear and providing a sense of stability in the midst of stress.

Let us acknowledge that Christians have faults. Many Christians' behavior is neurotic. Some of our conclusions are put forth in an intellectually sloppy manner. Many people do "use" religion solely as a crutch and an excuse for not tackling their problems responsibly. Some of our religious behavior and beliefs may be unconsciously motivated, and ungrounded in fact. We do have a tendency to make sweeping generalizations and to support our conclusions by the subjective experiences ("testimonies") of one or two persons. Too often we uncritically accept the pronouncements of preachers solely because they claim to be preaching "the Word." In these and similar areas, the psychological critics of religious experience clearly have raised some significant issues that we must consider seriously.

But the critics themselves often are guilty of bias, sweeping over-generalizations, selective perception, rigidity, ignoring data, and the unconscious or unexamined acceptance of antireligious presuppositions. Freud's stinging criticisms can be answered (see Collins, 1977), and so can the conclusions of Sargant (see Lloyd-Jones, 1959), as well as the arguments of those who discount miracles (see Lewis, 1947), and the challenges of others who seek to explain away religious experience.

As I have taught in seminaries for over ten years, I have not seen much theological or psychological interest in the psychology of religious experiences. Why are people religious? Why do we prefer different churches and seek different religious experiences? Why do some people have a healthy, mature religion (to use Allport's term, 1950), while others develop immature, neurotic belief systems and religious behavior? Surely Meehl and his colleagues are correct in concluding that one who does not come to terms with such religious experience issues as guilt, sin, conscience, and conversion (or, we might add, miracles, faith healing, demonism, glossolalia, and prayer) "cannot even begin to work out a cognitive rapprochement between Christian theology and the secular sciences of behavior" (1958, p. 5). Religious experience is a crucial problem area for psychological apologetics and for the integration of psychology and Christianity.

Public People-Helping

Several months ago, a respected colleague dropped by my office and asked if I would be interested in co-authoring a book on counseling through biblical preaching. I suggested that "Public People-Helping from the Pulpit" would be an apt title, and although we subsequently decided not to produce such a book, the suggestion did much to stimulate my thinking.

There are many people today who need help with personal problems, but who never see a counselor, never get any real pastoral help, and rarely even experience the comfort and guidance that can come from an understanding friend. At times there are no available counselors, but some avoid getting help because of insecurity, fear of rejection or ridicule, uncertainty, a theology that is critical of persons with problems, or a lack of funds. For these people, the only source of help may be what comes from books, popular articles, tapes, sermons, seminar presentations, radio and television programs, or other impersonal sources. Even those who do seek professional help with their problems have often been helped by articles or tapes that have been recommended by their counselors.

Closely aligned with these public approaches to people-helping are the self-help programs that currently are sweeping the country. In the United States alone, over half a million self-help groups, countless itinerant seminar speakers, and innumerable books and programs have appeared recently. There are organizations for alcoholics, drug addicts, gamblers, the aged, parents of the retarded, former mental patients, smokers, over-eaters, war veterans, suicide-prone people, women (and men) struggling with identity problems, parents without partners, and many more. We have programs that promise to bring effective speaking, weight loss, faster reading, greater assertiveness, parent effectiveness, and a host of other personal benefits. Books tell us how to be our own best friend, how to win over worry, how to be successful, and even how to overcome anxiety or to profit from stress.

There was a time in my professional career when I roundly criticized such popular approaches, dismissing them all as simplistic, easily misinterpreted, and potentially harmful. My opinion began to change when I saw that such public people-helping isn't always harmful. Sometimes it can be very helpful. Instead of criticizing or leaving the popular approaches to well-meaning, but psychologically naive, speakers and writers, we who are professionals must attempt to develop effective popular public approaches to complement the work of trained people-helpers.

Books and articles on the popular and self-help movements have only recently begun to appear (Gartner and Reissman, 1977; Katz and Bender, 1976), but even in this early stage of analysis we need to ask at least three questions: Why have the popular and self-help programs arisen? Are they effective? What relevance do they have to the issue of integration? (You will notice that I am focusing here on self-help programs as the most visible and currently popular example of public people-helping.)

Why self-help? For many years, people have turned for assistance to books, popular speakers, and neighbors. The self-help movement, therefore, isn't something unique to the 1970s and 1980s. Nevertheless, there seems to be a current surge of special interest in self-help, and it is interesting to speculate on the reasons for this. During the 1960s we experienced years of both social unrest and social concern. Civil rights, the antiwar movement, free speech, and the rise of the counterculture occupied our attention, as did the increase in crime, turmoil in the universities, decline in morality, and breakdown of the family unit. Many people apparently lost faith in the government, academia, science, and even the church. Perhaps there developed a mentality which assumed "if others can't help us, we'll have to help ourselves." Such self-help activities proved to be economical, apparently effective, and easily available. Coupled with this has been what one writer terms the current "American impulse to self-improvement" (Henninger, 1977). We are one of the richest nations in the world, but a nation of people who appear to be continually disenchanted with who we are. Restless and seeking for at least a temporary sense of security, stability, and hope, we have turned to one self-help approach after another. Many of these programs offer promises of quick success and this, of course, is also consistent with the mentality of our fast-paced society.

It would be comforting to assume that Christians are beyond all of this, able to rest in the Lord, and not be inclined to get caught up in self-help fads. Regrettably, this does not appear to be true. There is little, if anything, in the secular world that brings in crowds like the Gothard Seminars and similar movements. Christian book sales are at an all-time high, and some of the most popular books are those that offer practical help.

All this brings us to the disturbing conclusion, mentioned by several writers in the field (Gartner and Riessman, 1977; Greely, 1976; Henninger, 1977), that the rise of self-help movements may have come in response to a declining and apparently ineffective "old-time religion." The family, the neighborhood, the community, and the church appear to have lost much of their power. People are looking elsewhere for answers and help, and they respond quickly and enthusiatically to any promise of practical assistance, assured success, and specific formulae for action. Christians may be skeptical of a Dale Carnegie or an assertiveness-training program, but they easily embrace programs that are purportedly biblical, supported by testimonies to "prove" they work, and endorsed by fellow Christians or church leaders.

Is Self-Help Effective? The best answer to this question probably would be "sometimes." Much depends on the type of program, the way in which it is presented to the public, and the ability of an individual to stick with a program and to make it work. In a survey and investigation of several self-help programs, two researchers (Perri and Richards, 1977) reached some interesting conclusions: It *is* possible for us to help ourselves if we can stick with a program long enough to give it a chance to work, use techniques like self-monitoring to record progress and self-reward to motivate ourselves, or use a wide variety of approaches (so that if one method fails there are other methods we can continue to use). I suspect, in addition, that the most successful public people-helping comes to those who are stable enough to apply the principles of self-help without being overwhelmed by the demands of yet another "system" or pressure in life.

Of course there are dangers in any movement that encourages people to help themselves. Individuals in need of in-depth or specialized professional help may easily conclude that they can handle their own problems—but their problems will only get worse. If the individual fails to apply some formula for success, he or she may have the original problem compounded by a sense of guilt or inadequacy because of the failure. Most of us have seen such cripples following the latest popular seminar—especially if the leader has made exorbitant promises such as the one in a popular self-help book. "Of one thing I am confident," the author wrote. "You do not have to be depressed. . . . I am convinced that by using the formula in this book, you can avoid ever being depressed again." Such a promise can be devastating to the person who reads the book but remains depressed.

Is Self-Help Relevant to Integration? Both psychology and theology are concerned about helping people to mature, to face and successfully cope with problems, and to deal with the difficult questions of life. Once again, however, the secular psychologist and the Christian differ in their assumptions about how we deal with problems. Humanistic psychology, convinced of human potential and our independence from any supernatural force, assumes that individuals and groups must solve problems on their own. There was a song that expressed this many years ago. "Do you need a little help, could you use a little help?" the lyrics asked, and the reply was "I can handle this job all by myself, there's no help wanted!" In contrast, the Christian believes that he or she can "do all things," but only through Christ "who strengthens" us (Phil. 4:13). Christ may strengthen, sustain, and guide us through other brothers and sisters (or even through non-Christian professional helpers), but we assume that a personal God cares for us and intervenes in our lives. We are not alone in dealing with our problems.

Many of the same helping techniques are used in Christian and secular approaches to public helping or self-help. This is not surprising, since we all like to use methods that work. Nevertheless, it appears that some Christian speakers and writers criticize psychological techniques, redefine them in more religious terms, surround them with a Bible verse or two in order to give them respectability, and then advocate these "new" discoveries as if they were something unique.

The Christian interested in both psychology and theology must be more honest. And he or she must respond to at least three challenges in the area of public people-helping and the related self-help movement.

First, we must develop approaches to public people-helping (books, articles, spoken messages, and self-help programs) that clearly demonstrate our assumption that it is Christ who strengthens us, that the Lord sustains those who cast their burdens on him, and that the Word of God is powerful—even when it applies to human needs and problems. Talking about the power of God is cheap and empty, if it is not reflected in our lives, work and efforts to help others.

But our public help should also be psychologically sound. We should acknowledge the value of those many helping techniques that have been discovered and proven by our secular colleagues. At the same time, we must not advocate goals and techniques (regardless of their apparent effectiveness) that are inconsistent with biblical teachings. We must, in addition, make honest, realistic statements about the effectiveness of our public counseling and self-help methods—avoiding exorbitant claims of success. In addition, the development of such programs must involve both theological and psychological insights.

There is a second challenge for integration in the public people-helping area. We must help lay people, and psychologically untrained church leaders, to be selective in their acceptance of public advice and self-help programs.

Do you remember the people of Berea who are mentioned in Acts 17? They are described as "noble-minded" men and women, who listened carefully to the Apostle Paul and then went home to examine the Scriptures to see whether or not Paul's message was correct.

In the academic world we do this critical analysis all the time, but rarely is this so in the church. "If it comes from the pulpit or from a Christian book," many people assume, "it must be true," and testimonies or other personal experiences are accepted as proof of an idea's validity. To counteract this unthinking acceptance, we must show Christian lay persons how they can evaluate popular advice or public teaching.

But how can a lay person or church leader evaluate and be selective if he or she has not been encouraged or trained to be so? This training ought to start with people who have expertise both in theology and psychology. Such training, and the criticism of current popular Christian psychology, is necessary, even though it is not likely to be appreciated by people who want superficial explanations, how-to-do-it formulae, and easy answers.

We have left mention of the third, and perhaps most difficult, challenge to the end. We must grapple with the theological-psychological issue of whether the concept of self-help is even consistent with Christianity. The Bible encourages dependence on God and mutual support from others in the Body of Christ. There is no such thing as do-it-yourself Christianity, but neither do the Scriptures advocate an immature dependence or an attitude of waiting to be rescued.

Any Christian self-help approach, it seems, must acknowledge three fundamental assumptions. First, we are never really alone in our problems or our personal efforts at improvement. God, who is omniscient, omnipotent, and omnipresent, is also aware of our needs. He surely does help those who seek to help themselves. Second, we should acknowledge that God often works through the body of believers. This concept of the church as a healing community has been mentioned previously and is repeatedly emphasized in Scripture. Third, we must recognize the influence of biblical ethics. There are theological guidelines, mostly reducible to the concept of love, which must guide our actions—including our people-helping and our self-help. For example, self-help programs that teach us to assert power over others or to "look out for number one" can hardly be called Christian. These are self-centered and inconsistent with the biblical imperative of loving neighbors as ourselves.

Public people-helping rarely gets much attention in professional circles, but this may be one of the most crucial areas for consideration by those who are interested in the integration of psychology and theology.

Preventive People-Helping

When psychiatrist Gerald Caplan published *Principles of Preventive Psychiatry* (1964) the author issued a clear call for the helping professions to develop concern and programs for the prevention of personal problems. Of course few people are willing to pay a counselor's fee to get help in preventing a problem that has not yet arisen. People pay to get counseling for disturbing problems that already exist. Professional, pastoral, and peer helpers focus most of their attention on existing pain, and prevention often is relegated to the category of those issues that "we all should be concerned about—and will be if we ever have the time."

It is encouraging to realize that some people have taken the time to work on prevention, and this has become an important part of what we now know as the community mental-health movement. Certainly the church is an important part of the community and can have a significant bearing on whether problems develop or get worse. Premarital counseling, which was mentioned previously, helping a family cope with grief in a healthy way, developing creative programs for adolescents who might otherwise get into trouble, assisting older persons to anticipate and adjust to retirement—these are among the ways in which the church can get actively involved in prevention. In a creative book, published shortly after that of Caplan, Clinebell (1965) demonstrated that every ministry of the local church—worship, fellowship, administration, and youth programs, for example—can contribute to the mental health of the members and can lead to the prevention of problems. Westberg and Draper (1966) and Whitlock (1973) also addressed this issue, but to date no one has been excited enough about prevention in and through the church to give us clear motivation and direction on how this might be done.

A pastor commented to me not long ago on the recent appearance of so many books on church renewal. "Half of them are written by academic people who have never done anything to build or rebuild a church," he complained, probably with some justification. A similar charge might be hurled against any psychologist who attempts to tell churches what to do in the area of prevention. Every church is unique in some way, and headed by a pastor or pastoral staff with distinct personalities.

In spite of this, however, it would seem that people with expertise in psychology and theology—especially ecclesiology—could devote more time to determining how, in practical ways, the church can become a more loving community, which is concerned about healing and about the prevention of potential problems.

Conclusion

Any discussion of psychology and theology must conclude, I suggest, with a focus on the church. The Greek word *ekklesia,* which usually is translated "church" or "churches," appears 115 times in the New Testament and refers almost always to a group of believers. While the word sometimes appears to make reference to a "universal" body of Christians spread around the globe and across the centuries, the word more often applies to groups of believers who meet together in a local assembly. The New

Testament never classifies a building as a church. The "church" refers to people who are believers in Jesus Christ.

Before he ascended into heaven, Jesus gave final instructions to his followers, telling them to make disciples of all nations (Matt. 28:19-20). There was to be a twofold emphasis—evangelism and edification. In the opinion of many Bible scholars, God currently is working through His Holy Spirit to call people out of the world, introduce them to Jesus Christ, and bring new believers into the body for edification, growth, and fellowship.

As we are aware, the church over the years has deviated from these purposes. The witch hunts and crusades of earlier centuries hardly seem in keeping with the Great Commission, and more recently some of the political activities of church bodies have had, at best, shaky theological and biblical justification. Regrettably, psychology has also been a distracting force. The pastoral counseling movement, for example, has taken control of some churches so that evangelism and edification have slipped to second place, and counseling has become primary—a reversal that appears to contradict the biblical priorities.

In a penetrating article, written from his perspective as a priest and sociologist, Greeley (1976) notes that psychology has swept into the churches with such influence that in many places "therapy groups replace worship, encounter weekends substitute for retreats, sensitivity training replaces contemplation, and in some of the prayer houses of Catholic Pentecostalism, the techniques of behavior modification replace the holy rule and canon law as the glue that holds the community together. Freud has not substituted for Jesus, but Jesus begins to sound very much like Freud" (p. 225). The descriptive terms may be different, but much of this also describes modern Protestantism, including evangelicalism.

The term "relational theology" has been used to describe

a recent movement in the church that seeks to focus attention on people and interpersonal relations, rather than on the seemingly irrelevant points of theology. "Transactional theology," the more traditional emphasis on preaching and teaching about God's great transactions for humans and in human beings (e.g., the atonement, resurrection, justification, regeneration, sanctification), has not done much to help people with their personal problems. Pastors have found that Christians with solid theology are nevertheless unethical in their business practices, neurotic, unable to get along with people, experiencing divorce at an increasing rate, and struggling with problems of depression, anxiety, loneliness, or lack of sexual control. It is hardly surprising that, in frustration, if not desperation, many believers have turned to a more psychologically astute relational theology, which claims to be built on the Bible, but is sensitive to human needs.

This is a very crucial issue for those interested in integration, because relational theology, while largely resulting from an apparent failure in transactional theology, also appears to have been prompted by the recent explosion of interest in psychology. It is not surprising, therefore, that the influence of psychology in the church and the rise of relational theology have become cause for both debate and alarm in many Christian circles (see, for example, Barber, Colwell, and Strauss, 1975; Smith, 1975).

Ramm (1972) has cited some of the dangers of transactional theology—dangers I believe psychologists, theologians, church leaders, and lay persons should seek to overcome without throwing out either the great theological doctrines or the insights of contemporary psychology.

Danger 1: The truth in transactional theology may be lost. We are saved by the "mighty works and wonders and signs" (Acts 2:22) of God. Interpersonal (transactional) theology must be built upon the great transactions.

> Danger 2: The concern for the psychological may eventually displace Christian truth and Christian concerns. The pastor may become a pulpit psychologist and cease to be a minister of the Word of God.
>
> Danger 3: The concern for the psychological may convert us into humanists where all our values are psychological and humanitarian and all significant Christian values and perspectives are defined out of existence (p. 22).[10]

Perhaps these dangers, especially the last one, are more apparent than real, but they do give us reason for serious reflection.

Psychology is here to stay. It is a field of study through which all of us—in and out of the church—can achieve greater understanding of ourselves and others, and greater effectiveness in people-helping. Certainly there are problems, untruths, and antibiblical aspects of the field. We, as Christians, cannot accept and embrace the findings of psychology uncritically. Neither can we give assent to the full-scale psychologizing of the church. The Christian and the church have been commanded to make disciples. This is our prime responsibility, but as part of that responsibility we must edify one another and reach out to help one another. Psychology, tested against the Scriptures and utilized in the service of the church, can, and I believe is, being used by the Holy Spirit to help the church maintain its primary function.

I resist a transactional theology that has no practical relevance. I also resist any relational theology that has no biblical foundation. Both are unbalanced. What we need is a theology and church that are solidly based on Scripture and on the great transaction doctrines, but sensitive to the

---

[10]From Bernard Ramm, "Is It Safe to Shift to 'Interpersonal Theology'?" Reprinted by permission of *Eternity* Magazine, copyright 1972, Evangelical Ministries, Inc., 1716 Spruce Street, Philadelphia, PA 19103.

needs of people who are hurting, struggling, lost, and in need of Christ's healing and help. To move in this direction should, I submit, be the goal of Christian psychologists and theologians alike. It is at the crux of this whole topic of integration.

A Personal Postscript

Writing these paragraphs and pondering their content has for me been a challenging time of reflection and reevaluation. I am committed intellectually to the task of integration. I want it to be reflected in my work, my writing, and my teaching. Most of all, however, I want my theology and my psychology to be integrated in my life—not compartmentalized into separate noninteracting categories. This is a lofty, largely unattainable goal; to have a life-style that shows one's commitment to Jesus Christ and one's personal application of biblical *and* psychological principles. My family, my close friends, and especially I, know how easy it is for me to fall short of this ideal. In addition, my talking about this might alert others to my failures; but I add this postscript for a very important reason. I believe that the integration of psychology and theology is an important intellectual challenge. I believe that integration must have practical applications. But I believe even more that integration must start and be reflected in the mind and behavior of the integrator.

CHAPTER 4

Integration: The Adjoiners

H. Newton Malony

The dictionary defines "adjoin" as meaning "is near enough to touch" and gives as an example, "Canada adjoins the United States." The thoughts in this chapter are not those of Gary Collins. They are "adjoiners." In other words, they are the comments of several scholars who were "touched by" Collins' ideas and who have chosen to respond to them. These are not messages from distant lands. Rather, they are interactive "adjoiners." We affirm the thrust of Collins' model, but we choose to critique it constructively in hopes of broadening its borders and enriching its import. We are indeed "near enough to touch" but different enough to be noteworthy.*

These comments will address the following issues:

Would a reconsideration, in socio-cultural terms, of the nature of biblical authority enchance the possibility of more meaningful integration between psychology and theology?

To what sort of contemporary problems could efforts at integration be addressed?

---

*This chapter includes a collation of responses to Collins' lectures by a missionary anthropologist, a pastoral theologian, a clinical psychologist, and a graduate student.

Are there optional models for interrelating psychology and theology that should be considered?

Can integration be practically illustrated in an explicit psychotherapeutic paradigm?

The Socio-Cultural Perspective*

Collins suggested that psychology and theology are "two separate and unique fields shedding light on our understanding of similar issues." Although he would, without doubt, grant the importance of the environment in which persons live, he does not mention it, and by this omission implicitly discounts the influence of culture.

Many scholars would agree that there is no way to integrate the perspectives of psychology and theology and come up with an adequate understanding of human behavior. Such an integration would be inadequate, because it overlooks a fundamental premise; namely, that man is a culture-bound being. The state of the inner psyche is not only a reflection of disorientation from God and essential self-centeredness, but is also a mirror of the social milieu.

Anthropology is the "sleeper" that Collins forgets. Only as psychology and theology are informed by anthropology will integration at more than a provincial level be possible. "Mind" is not a ready-made entity—a thing full-formed at birth. Rather, mind is a formation, a product of social forces. All human behavior is culturally variable rather than constant. When one omits the anthropological perspective, one falls prey to the temptation to make

---

*These comments include ideas and quotations from Arthur F. Glasser's "Integration Is Impossible If God Speaks with Two Voices," mimeographed, Fuller Theological Seminary, Pasadena, CA, 1978. Used with permission.

Figure 7

A HINDU INTEGRATION MODEL

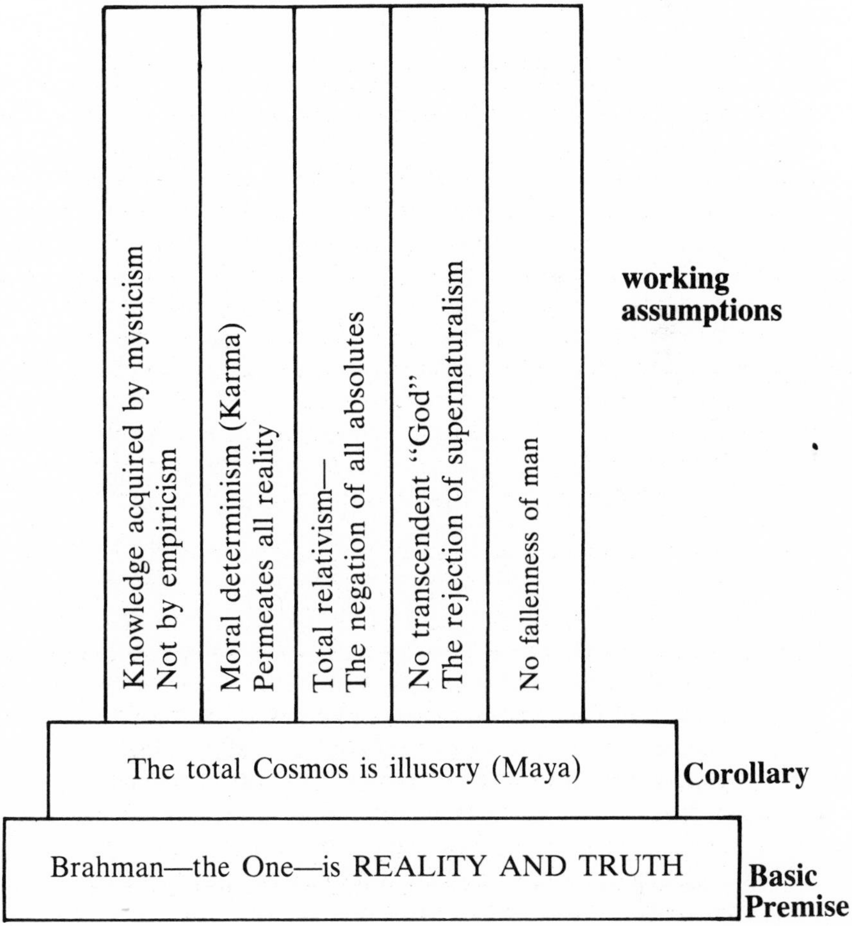

Knowledge acquired by mysticism
Not by empiricism

Moral determinism (Karma)
Permeates all reality

Total relativism—
The negation of all absolutes

No transcendent "God"
The rejection of supernaturalism

No fallenness of man

**working
assumptions**

The total Cosmos is illusory (Maya)   **Corollary**

Brahman—the One—is REALITY AND TRUTH   **Basic
Premise**

sweeping generalizations about the human condition that obtain only among a minority of the human race.

For example, Hindus might accept Collins' basic premise about God—whom they would identify as Brahman. But they could easily demonstrate the utter consistency of building thereon an entirely different set of corollaries and working assumptions. Figure 7 illustrates this alternative.

It can easily be noted that this differs radically from the model on page thirty-four that clearly comes out of a dualistic Western intellectual tradition.

The real crux of the issue is the manner in which Collins uses the Bible in his paradigm. He states that God has spoken "through the Bible (disclosed truth) and nature (discovered truth)." However, it is not very helpful to speak of God as the source of all truth, if the truth that comes from God through the Bible is differentiated from the truth that comes from either psychology or anthropology. Perhaps the following diagram can make this distinction clear.

Figure 8 reiterates what has been said about the incompleteness that inevitably results when one integrates only the perspectives of theology and psychology. If anthropological data is also admitted, one might theoretically argue that a real integration takes place where the three circles overlap. A faulty assumption is deliberately included in this diagram. Note that the empirical data supplied by psychology is the result of much controlled observation of Western man. And the empirical data supplied by anthropology is also the result of similar controlled observation of individuals, societies, and cultures worldwide. Obviously, the mastery of this empirical data (whether from psychology or anthropology) is influenced to no small degree by the intuition of the experienced observer, the free use of his reasoning and

Figure 8

THE COLLINS MODEL

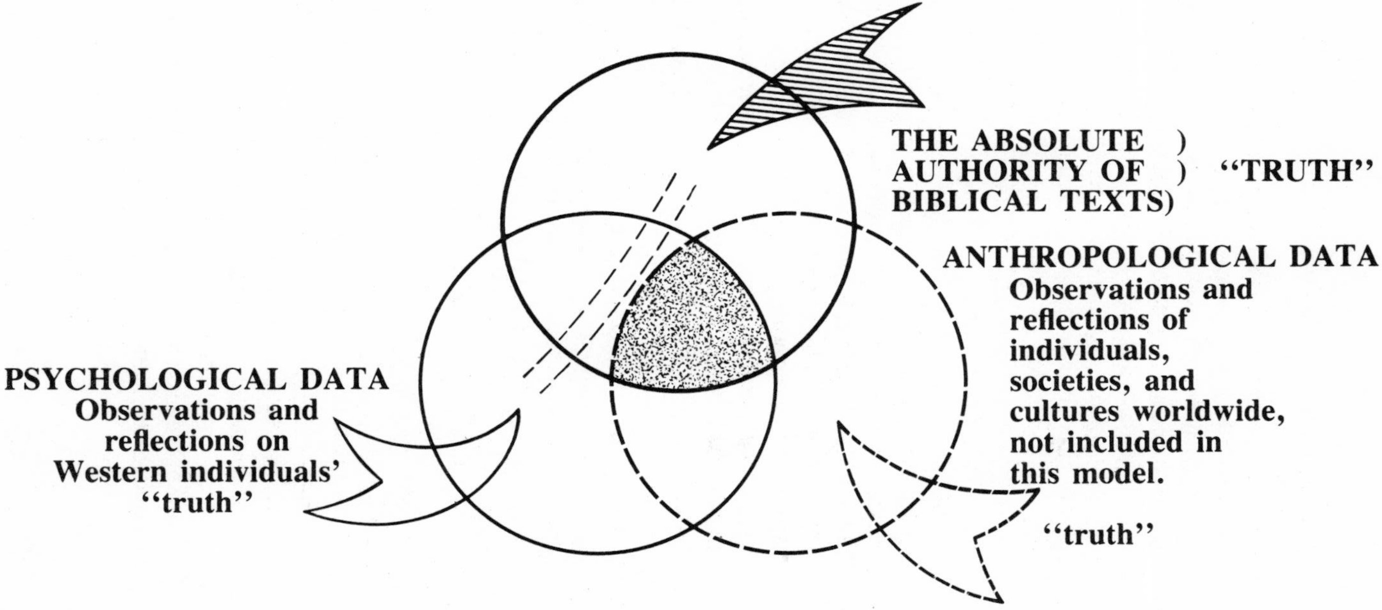

THE ABSOLUTE
AUTHORITY OF
BIBLICAL TEXTS)
} "TRUTH"

ANTHROPOLOGICAL DATA
Observations and
reflections of
individuals,
societies, and
cultures worldwide,
not included in
this model.

"truth"

PSYCHOLOGICAL DATA
Observations and
reflections on
Western individuals'
"truth"

associative powers, and the authority of the steadily accumulating data.

But tension enters the integrative process when the Bible is also included in the "data bank." This tension is inevitable if, as Collins maintains, the witness of the Bible is to be regarded differently from any data gathered through research and observation. In his desire to maintain evangelical authenticity and orthodoxy, Collins keeps affirming the supremacy of Scripture. He states, "The Bible is our primary resource against which all other facts must be tested." All data must be "biblically oriented." The Scriptures are "a firm core around which all psychological activities can be centered and against which we can test our psychological conclusions and techniques." "Scripture should be a standard." We must carefully weed out "those elements in psychology that oppose the Scriptures."

The following diagram indicates this relationship between the Bible and psychology.

Here is an attempt to describe the type of integration Collins advocates. He distinguishes "TRUTH" from "truth," and recognizes that because the various data under examination are from different sources (some revealed and the other empirical), tension is bound to exist between Christian and non-Christian psychologists. In this model, the Bible represents God's authority, and is, like God, outside the flow of history. Its propositions and texts are not culturally conditioned; they are outside the context of experience and can only descend with a heavy wham into the integration process he advocates.

Collins seems to be wedded to the increasingly popular, but highly debatable, thesis that Scripture is composed of revelatory propositions. "The Bible is a collection of sentences—each one with the label 'TRUTH' and each proposition a self-contained, infallible revelation. The Word of God is reduced to Bible texts a fallible person can infallibly use. This Word is a complex set of rules for our

Figure 9

GOD SPEAKS WITH TWO TYPES OF VOICES

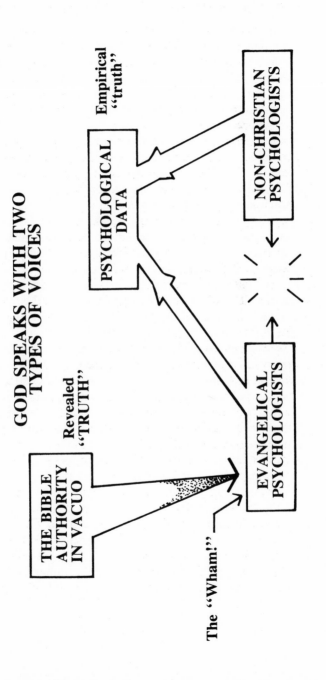

faith and conduct, admittedly given to the Israelites (in the Old Testament) and to certain sections of the apostolic church (in the New Testament) but which are not related to any existing culture today."

Actually, Scripture points beyond itself to God. It is canonical, an authoritative rule. But "the new creation" is the rule by which Christians are called to walk (Gal. 6:16). In the Scriptures the Holy Spirit bears witness to the word of God. But this does not mean that we have the right to read the Bible from an a-historical, a-cultural perspective. The anthropologist reminds us that the Bible itself is culturally conditioned. Nothing in it is universal in the sense of being above or outside culture. Only God is the Absolute, the Supracultural, the Ultimate. And he has disclosed himself in Scripture through his mighty acts on behalf of his people. More, he has given intimations of what these acts were meant to disclose of his person and purpose. In so acting and speaking, God accommodated himself to the forms and meaning that made sense to his people in their particular time and culture.

This means that if we would know today the essence of the biblical revelation, we must give ourselves to the difficult and demanding exegetical task of discovering how God's deeds and words were understood by those to whom they first came. We must then translate this understanding into formulations and explanations that make sense to his people today, within their own cultural frames of reference. Since, at best, we are terribly flawed by the Fall, we desperately need the illumination of the Holy Spirit to guide us as we become involved in this exegesis and translation. Even then, we will only see "as through a glass darkly," and our knowledge will be at best, "in part" (I Cor. 13:12). Whereas we have confidence that the Bible is our infallible rule of faith and conduct, we must not presume to regard ourselves as infallible in our use of the Bible. Indeed, our understanding of the Bible is not unlike the understanding that the psychologist has of the data he has gathered through his empirical research. As he is not infallible in his use of this data, neither are we infallible in our understanding or application of Scripture.

The Bible, therefore, does not seek to convey its authority by texts. Texts are but empirical data, and Christians are called to experience their "true" truth through encounter with God. Only through establishing existential touch with Jesus as he is disclosed in the Bible does the Christian begin to enter into the Bible's authority.

In summary, note Figure 10.

Figure 10

GOD SPEAKS WITH ONE VOICE

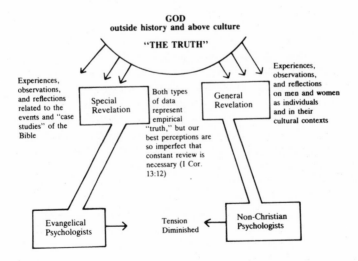

Reading the Bible is an experiential activity not unlike the psychologist's research in the laboratory. Only if the evangelical psychologist approaches the Bible this way will he have an authority comparable to the authority the non-Christian psychologist derives from his careful observation and accumulated experience of the human scene. Only thereby will God be found speaking with one voice, in both special and general revelation. Indeed, this larger data base will inevitably invalidate certain of the non-Christian perspectives on psychology. Furthermore, our continuing examination of the empirical data of Scripture will cause us also to put aside as invalid many of the theological perspectives that we earlier regarded as infallible.

Thus, the corrective of a socio-cultural perspective is a radical one. It makes possible a manner of integration that is quite impossible where only psychology and theology are considered. We think such socio-cultural addition is essential. At least here God speaks with *one* voice and the sacred/secular split is overcome.

The Contemporary Problem*

In his earlier book (1977), Collins seems to suggest that the current issues to which integration should be addressed are a bankrupt psychology, a self-satisfied theology, and a monolithic science grounded in questionable assumptions.

Collins suggests that modern science assumes the validity of empiricism (we can believe only what we experience); relativism (instead of absolute standards, propositions, and

---

*These comments include ideas and quotations from Robert N. Schaper's "Complementarity and Integration," mimeographed, Fuller Theological Seminary, Pasadena, CA, 1978, used with permission; and Timothy Weber's "Coincidence of Opposites: the Meeting of Psychology and Theology," mimeographed, Fuller Theological Seminary, Pasadena, California, 1978, used with permission.

beliefs, truth varies with the observer's social situation and perspective); reductionism (all behavior can be explained in terms of smaller units); and naturalism (humanity is sovereign, and all behavior is the result of natural forces).

It is important to call attention to these presuppositions and to note that they are often overlooked. However, it is another thing to presume that all scientists function within these philosophical parameters or that they naïvely accept them without question. This is by no means true of all psychologists, as Havens (1977) has so poignantly noted. To take such a position is to caricature modern science and to engage in yet another form of "spoiling the Egyptians," an approach to integration Collins discounts. To ignore the fact that many scientists (natural and behavioral as well as social) are reconsidering their assumptions, is to deny oneself allies one might otherwise have.

For example, new considerations in the study of biology, especially sociobiology, open wide the discussion of determinism. There is increasing unwillingness to assume that man has no control over his "evolutionary development." With no pretense of any religious motivation, Jonas Salk suggests a grand scheme for understanding the development of mankind. He proposes that we are now moving into "Epoch B." This new epoch is the era of "wisdom." The evolutionary characteristic of Epoch A was "fitness," which will not be discarded, but will be superseded by wisdom. The movement is not inexorable. In fact, it is modifiable. It may or may not take place, and that is part of "nature's game." All this is to emphasize that there is dissatisfaction among biologists with the idea that genetic inheritance is merely through blind chance, or that humankind cannot qualify to take over its own evolutionary process. We are more controlled by our genes than we realize. Yet our genetic instructions offer a "framework of opportunity" rather than an inexorable, programmed scenario. Genetic traits are manifested in appropriate circumstances, and biological development seems to depend on an interplay between genetics and environment. This means that ecobiology and psychology have their influence on the whole question of freedom as it relates to genetic determinism. The work of Loren Eiseley *(The Immense Journey)* and Albert Rosenfeld *(The Second Genesis: The Coming Control of Life)* shows that the problem of determinism has not been closed, even by the scientific community. The removal of determinism as a psychological presupposition—on scientific rather than religious grounds—is a consummation devoutly to be wished by those who would work for the integration of psychology and theology.

Another example is the erosion of materialistic monism. This is taking place in the unlikely area of physics, which has traditionally been the "hard" ideal of the scientific disciplines. It has seemed the most objective and precise of the sciences, and psychology and the social sciences have seemed "soft" in comparison. Now quantum mechanics and the relativity theory have allowed physics to become an introduction to a kind of knowledge that seems genuinely mystical. Atomic physics now tells us that the basic stuff of our universe, the sub-atomic particles, do not exist with certainty at definite places, but rather show "tendencies to exist." They become waves—like patterns of probabilities. All this is to say that there are not any "building blocks," but rather a web of relationships between the various parts of a unified whole.

The nature of mind is mysterious, but this no longer seems out of place. The atomic physicist is equally mystifying when he describes an atom. If an atom were blown up to the size of the Houston Astrodome, the nucleus would be the size of a grain of salt! The atom itself is small beyond comprehension. If an orange were blown up to be the size of the earth, the atoms of the orange would be the size of cherries. In such a world, the intuitive mind becomes as necessary as the rational faculties, and our Western world view has not reached such a dynamic balance. But again it should be noted that determinism can be questioned by means of scientific methodology, not merely by one's moving it aside in favor of divine revelation.

More important, perhaps, than his neglect of allies in the scholarly community who are also questioning the traditional scientific values, is Collins' tendency to analyze the contemporary situation predominantly in terms of basic theory, rather than practical existence. The issues for the average person are existential and personal, not theoretical. A helpful complement to Collins' thinking would be Gilkey's (1969) analysis of the secular mood that dominates the modern scene. The facets of this profile make sense of the tendency of numerous persons to resist, or to evidence little interest in, integration.

Gilkey (*contra* Collins) suggests that these elements of secularism are (1) culturally pervasive and not just localized within science, and (2) in the foreground of people's self-understanding and not merely background presuppositions of life. They are: contingency, relativity, temporality, and autonomy.

Contingency: This is the condition of being subject to chance. True, the flow of events once in a while might have some predictable order, often in an assurance given to us by the "sciences" (for example, the nightly weather reports, inflation theory, child-rearing practices). But whatever order or assurance we have concerning "the way it is" has evolved in time and will change in time. While there might be *causes* for events. (causes we are often unaware of), there are no *reasons* for these occurrences; they happen only by chance.

Contingency, therefore, is experienced as fate. Faith might try to give order to fate on occasion, especially when we experience more questions and ambiguity about our lives than we care to bear. Nevertheless, there is an absence of coherence in many lives, which may be an important reason why psychology is necessary. Focusing as psychology does on the concrete and observable—the "facts"—gives people an opportunity to ground themselves on some kind of "truth." For example, the careful attention given to the tracking and recording of problem behaviors, and the carefully planned schedule of reinforcers for small increments in behavior change that are all part of a "behavior modification program" (Watson and Tharp, 1972), may be seen in part as a cultural answer to an essentially theological problem: How do people find some semblance of coherence and control in a contingent world?

Relativity: Gilkey's second characteristic of contemporary life, central to the secular spirit, is relativity. Collins has also noted that relativism is a component of psychology (1977, pp. 82-84). We are not only evolving, but "unnerved" by the fast pace of social change and the rapid obsolescence of things, people, and ideas that give only brief meaning to our lives. Relativism implies that there are no absolutes, no permanency, no fixed authority. The emphasis, says Gilkey, is on "change as opposed to sameness and identity, process as opposed to substance, becoming as opposed to being, and context as opposed to innate individual capacities and powers" (1969, p. 49).

This last point is reflected especially in psychology's emphasis on the social context as the primary shaper of the personality, as in Rotter's social learning theory: "The first assumption of social learning theory is that the unit of investigation for the study of the personality is the interactions of the individual and his meaningful environment" (Rotter and Hochreich, 1975, p. 94). Gilkey also says that the relativist "seeks to understand the individual and his behavior, not in terms of his individual, changeless substance and soul, but in terms of the nexus of social relations out of which he has been formed and so in terms of which he is to be explained" (p. 49). As Collins correctly asserts, this relativism creates a situation where absolute truth appears to be unattainable (1977, p. 84). Thus, as Gilkey suggests, there doesn't seem to be any basis for religious belief in the absolute or sacred, or an ultimate ground beyond the shifting, immediately given.

Temporality: Gilkey defines this characteristic of contemporary culture as "becoming, all is changing, all is in passage, out of the past and into the future, and so all effects come and go—and all is mortal—and nothing else is real" (p. 54). Collins uses no comparable category to describe psychology *per se,* although his category of "relativism" might speak to this flow of things and effects (1977, p. 82). In his analysis of "psychology as selfism," Vitz points out how contemporary psychology, with its emphasis on experience, has moved into the culture. An example is the Erhard Seminar Training where the main goal is to get the participants to "transform their ability to *experience* living" (1977, p. 32). Harvey Cox has noted that this same emphasis on experiencing the immediate is a prime reason why many people have become enamored with the neo-Oriental religious revival (1977). This cultural concentration on developing oneself, process, becoming, immediacy, experience—endemic to our way of living—characterizes "temporality."

What happens, then, to a theology grounded in the eternal verities of the past? Is there anything credible that transcends all the "passages" of life we are now so inclined to discuss and analyze (Sheehy, 1974)? Collins recognizes that this experiential dimension is often a part of psychology, even of theological training (p. 45). However, the phenomenon is much more broadly based. This temporality is part of our culture's self-understanding and therefore calls for more than the "flexing of scriptural muscles" in protest as Collins might suggest.

Autonomy: This characteristic of man in our culture most closely parallels Collins' description of psychology as "naturalistic," meaning that "man is alone" and that what he becomes is a function of his own abilities (1977, p. 88). If just contingency, relativity, and temporality were to characterize culture, the picture would be grim indeed. Our culture attempts to use a sense of autonomy to encourage whatever optimism is possible. Because there is little confidence in a relative, transient world; autonomy, according to Gilkey, establishes the person's right to "know his own truth, to decide about his own existence, to create his own meanings, and to establish his own values" (p. 58). The opposition between creative autonomy and religion (e.g., Karl Marx) has been a recurrent theme in philosophy and religion. Should the theological response to secular, psychological thought be Collins' simple assertion that "God exists and is the source of all truth" (1977 p. 22)? The cultural pervasiveness of, not only autonomy, but the other characteristics of culture, demands a more complex and personal response than seems apparent in Collins' model.

The issue here is a redefinition of the problem to which integration addresses itself.

Optional Models for Integration*

The third question to which this essay is addressed is, Are there optional models for integrating psychology and theology that should be considered? The answer is, perhaps.

Earlier in this volume, Collins listed six possible approaches to integration. The main difficulty behind this discussion of "approaches" is that methodologies of integration are mixed with attitudes toward integration.

---

*These comments include ideas and quotations from Timothy Weber's "Coincidence of Opposites: The Meeting of Psychology and Theology," mimeographed, Fuller Theological Seminary, Pasadena, CA, 1978, used with permission.

For example, Collins cites Paul Tournier as a practitioner of the "denial approach," which asserts that the conflict between psychology and theology is more fictional than real. The "approach" seems to be more of an attitude toward integration than a methodology. In contrast, Collins cites Richard Bube's work as an example of the "levels of analysis approach," which explains that psychology and theology view the universe from two different perspectives, with different levels; both psychology and science describe different facets of reality than does theology (p. 24). The description of Bube's work seems to focus more on methodology while echoing the same nonconflict attitude of Tournier.

The point is that although a person's attitude toward integration will affect the choice of a methodology, attitude is not the same as methodology. A basically positive attitude toward the meeting of psychology and theology may utilize several methodologies (e.g., Collins' "levels of analysis" or "integrated models" approaches). Reuel Howe, in his *The Miracle of Dialogue* (1963), makes this same point when he says "It may be necessary to distinguish between the *principle* of dialogue and dialogue as a *method.* . . . Any method of communication may be servant of the dialogical principle," which means being alert to the "meanings" and situations of the hearers (p. 40). Howe gives scant attention to methods of communication, but accents the prime importance of the attitudes that people bring to the communication process. This same type of perspective may be applied to the project of integration where methodological considerations are secondary to the attitudes and expectations that people bring to this project. Therefore, in any consideration of "prospects for integration," the first stage of analysis should be focused on attitudes rather than methods. Prospects for this integration project probably depend more on the different types of attitudes than on the methods people bring to the task.

Figure 11

INDEX-ing Attitudes Toward the Meeting of Psychology and Theology

SYNTHETICAL POSITIONS			*ANTITHETICAL POSITIONS*	
INTEGRATIVE ATTITUDE	NULLIFICATION ATTITUDE	DIALOGICAL ATTITUDE	ERISTICAL ATTITUDE	XENOPHOBIC ATTITUDE
(I)	(N)	(D)	(E)	(X)

CATALOGING COLLINS' APPROACHES

"Integrated Models" (Carter & Mohline)	"Denial" (Tournier) "Levels of Analysis" (Bube)	"Railroad Track" (Meehl, et al.)	"Spoiling the Egyptians" (Crabb) "Rebuilding" (Collins)	"Confrontational" (Adams)

While attitudes do, in part, determine the methods one might consider using, people can be categorized by a particular attitude, even when they use different methodologies.

Below is a scheme for understanding the different attitudes toward the meeting of psychology and theology. These five different attitudes are represented by the acronym INDEX: Integrative attitude, Nullification attitude, Dialogical attitude, Eristical attitude, and Xenophobic attitude.

These attitudes appear on a scale, the left of which (integrative attitude) represents the *synthetical* position toward psychology and theology (unification of the two disciplines), and the right of which (xenophobic attitude) represents the *antithetical* position toward psychology and theology (disengagement of the two disciplines). This attitudinal analysis would appear to be more important when discussing prospects for integration than would be first discussing different methodologies of integration. Thus, persons working in this field of psychology and theology might be "catalogued" according to two variables, attitude and methodology.

"I" is for the integrative attitude: The word "integration" is usually the term evangelical Christians use to refer to this project of working in the interface of psychology and theology. The Fuller Graduate School of Psychology has one part of its curriculum, usually considered the curriculum's "unique feature," that is devoted to the integration of psychology and theology. The *Journal of Psychology and Theology,* published by the Rosemead Graduate School of Professional Psychology, identifies itself as "an evangelical forum for the integration of psychology and theology."

Perhaps Farnsworth is stating a primary assumption behind the integrative attitude when he says, "It is shown that with an uncontaminated conduct of inquiry across the levels of inquiry, psychology and Christianity can become substantially integrated in a way that promotes unity and includes wholeness of truth" (1974, p. 116). The chief postulate of Collins' "integrated models approach," represented by the work of Carter and Mohline, appears to be the synthetic assertion that psychology and theology can be unified: "All truth is God's truth, therefore, the truths of psychology (general revelation) are neither contradictory nor contrary to revealed truth (special revelation) but are integrative in a harmonious whole" (Collins, 1977, p. 16). Carter and Mohline are aware of different epistemologies, foci of explanations, and levels of explanation in psychology and theology, but still push toward a comfortable synthesis.

This attitude is problematic in several respects. First, the term "integration" connotes a static, meshed fit between psychology and theology, whereas the meeting between psychology and theology appears to be more dynamic. As a worker in this field, Paul Tillich often described himself as "on the boundary," a term Collins uses to describe working in this area. In a recent paper, William Rogers uses Tillich's description to picture his own work in psychology and theology: "To stay on such a boundary is both precarious and potentially immensely creative, but it is also at times lonely and a bit ill defined, because in a classical sense, we are neither strict psychologists nor strict theologians" (1977, p. 1). Ambiguity, tension, and precariousness, are better descriptions of working in both psychology and theology, disciplines that have so little, but so much, in common. The implication behind this integrative attitude is that where a fit is welded, integration is achieved, and where no fit is possible, integration is unrealized.

Second, this implied expectation of a fit may either discourage would-be integrators who find a fit to be impossible, or it may cause integrators to force a fit without being sensitive to the differences in presuppositions, content, and methodologies in psychology and theology. Thus, integration becomes somewhat of an artificial project and, more important, its pursuit might sacrifice valuable dialogue and confrontations between these two disciplines.

Third, this forced enmeshment of psychology and theology may have undesirable theological ramifications, even for those Christians, such as Helmut Thielicke (1974), who are not closed fundamentalists, but culturally open in their approach. Thielicke cautions against this facile generalization that speaks of a unity of "God's truth and man's truth" in the world, with the Bible acting as the norm for judging other truth: "one cannot treat the relation between God and man as a systematic entity. There is between the reality of God and that of the world an ontological distinction which does not permit us to understand them as dimensions of one and the same reality" (p. 366).

"N" is for the nullification attitude: This attitude moves away from the synthetic, integrative attitude that seeks a fit between psychology and theology. Instead the attitude is expressed in this way: "Psychology and theology do not need to be fit together. There is no real conflict, but compatibility. Each discipline looks at the same reality from a different perspective. And both work together in helping troubled people." Here psychology and theology do not need to be meshed together because there is no tension or conflict. The tension is nullified and the disciplines cooperate; working together and suggesting "truths" about reality from different levels of analysis. Collins' discussion of Tournier (who sees no conflict from the clinical viewpoint) and his description of Bube's approach (who sees no conflict from the theoretical viewpoint) are two examples of this same nullification attitude, but there are two different areas of interest, or, possibly, two different methodologies operating.

The benefit of this attitude is that a serious effort is made to use both psychology and theology profitably. However, as it was suggested above, those who might adopt this synthesizing attitude may be, in part, compensating for a long history of antiscientific diatribes from the religious community. Furthermore, I believe Collins is correct in criticizing Tournier's approach as a clinical "oversimplification" (p. 12). The same criticism can be charged to Bube's "levels of analysis" approach. Nullification of conflict overlooks the different views concerning the nature of personhood, and the methodological differences regarding how we come to know about ourselves and the world. The nullification attitude approaches psychology and theology with conciliation, but without a sensitivity to "being on the boundary." There seems to be little awareness of the tension of living in a secular world where self-understanding is primarily psychological in character, and theological language is rejected as meaningless, not simply accepted as "another level of reality."

"D" is for the dialogical attitude: The word "dialogue" means an "exchange of ideas and opinions" *(Webster's Seventh New Collegiate Dictionary,* 1967, s.v.). If the evangelical community has used the word "integration" to describe its efforts toward bringing about a meeting between psychology and theology, the more moderate/liberal sectors of Protestantism have used the word "dialogue" to describe their work in this field. The collection of essays by representatives from the Divinity School of the University of Chicago entitled *The Dialogue Between Theology and Psychology* (Homans, 1968) is an example of this attitude at work, an attitude that capitalizes on "creative interchange" and mutual stimulation (Brauer, 1968), while realizing the "hazard" of being "on the boundary lines between disciplines" (Homans, 1968). Another excellent reference that depicts the dialogical attitude in action is *Psychology and Religion: A Contemporary Dialogue,* a commentary by Joseph Havens, and

edited conversations between nine leading psychologists, a philosopher, and two theologians (1968).

Although there is the danger of never going beyond the "exploratory" stage with this attitude, the approach provides a tentativeness mixed with the tenacity of encounter, a recognition of being precariously on the boundary between psychology and theology, a struggle with the differing presuppositions and methodologies, and an overall commitment to conversation. An important component here is the awareness that the conversants need to be, not only critical about each other, but also self-critical about the inadequacies of their own respective traditions and symbols. Psychologists need to examine carefully the inherent problems and shortcomings in their work, and theologians need to be sensitive to the inadequacies of their "theologies."

This self-critical component is most important for the dialogical attitude because, from the theological perspective, it leaves the possibility open that psychology may not only *help* theology in assessing the nature of man (as Collins admits), but that psychology may also *correct* theology. This "correction" resembles Gilkey's viewpoint (from a psychological perspective), that although theology may be valid, it does not make connections with felt, lived experience. Perhaps orthodox theology has been too busy *answering* culture's attack when it should have been asking questions and evaluating the needs and symbols expressed by culture.

"E" is for the eristical attitude: The word "eristic" comes from a Greek word that means "fond of wrangling" *(Webster's Seventh New Collegiate Dictionary,* 1967, s.v.). The eristical attitude is characterized by disputatious, argumentative reasoning debating the validity of other assertions to the "one truth." On the spectrum of attitudes noted in the figure, the eristical attitude, falling on the right side of the median, begins to take the general tone of an

antagonistic relationship with psychology. Psychology is considered useful, espcially in practical people-helping matters, but must be carefully screened and contended with on the theoretical level.

Both Collins' description of Crabb's approach, which he calls "spoiling the Egyptians," and Collins' own "rebuilding" approach reflect the eristical attitude toward the meeting of psychology and theology. Crabb's term "spoiling the Egyptians" is borrowed from the Old Testament description of the Israelites taking from their oppressors what was needed for their trip through the wilderness. Presumably, then, theology takes what it can use from psychology while carefully "weeding out of those elements in psychology that oppose the Scriptures." Rather than an emphasis on listening to psychology, the emphasis here is on using psychology and testing it against the criterion of "infallible, inspired, inerrant revelation."

With a strict, non-self-critical insistence on the truth of Scripture, Crabb places himself in a basically argumentative, defensive posture vis-á-vis psychology.

Likewise, Collins is intent on "rebuilding" psychology on the *sine qua non* of God's truth and the assumptions that follow, such as biblical absolutism and Christian supernaturalism. For example, Collins asserts that "biblical absolutes" can be found to guide behavior and that the "supernatural" has important implications for behavior. Collins seldom qualifies his assertions. His position appears to be unequivocal. And his interest seems to be merely in the assertion against psychology of truths which, by virtue of belonging to the Christian tradition, are true. Theology needs to attend better to its own problems with expression and symbolic representation and to listen more carefully to the secular world, where the primary symbols of meaning are psychological.

A firm grounding in the Christian faith is important in working in this interdisciplinary field (we can thank Collins for reinforcing this notion). However, a non-self-critical emphasis on scriptural authority, the defensive assertion of Scripture's internal validity without attending to the question of external validity (meaning), and the insensitivity to psychology's and culture's problems with theology, can only generate an eristical debate about conflicting presuppositions that leads to no real solution.

"X" is for the xenophobic attitude: The word "xenophobia" is defined as "fear and hatred of strangers or foreigners or of anything that is strange or foreign" *Webster's Seventh New Collegiate Dictionary,* 1967, s.v.). In this field of psychology and theology—from the theological vantage point—xenophobia is an aversion to psychology and a withdrawal into theological categories that are defended as the only true, meaningful symbols of existence. The eristical attitude also falls toward the antithetical end of the spectrum, but still maintains a conversation, albeit an argumentative one, with psychology (clinical tools are used with censure). On the other hand, the xenophobic attitude pushes for a complete dissociation from psychology on both the theoretical and practical levels, epitomizing the antithesis between psychology and theology.

In his array of approaches, Collins does not have one that typifies this attitude. However, elsewhere in his lectures (pp. 6, 42) he refers to Adams, Gothard, and La Haye, practical theologians who see no need to bring psychology into their systems. In fact, Adams dismisses psychology as harmful, irrelevant, helpless, and hopeless. Needless to say, this attitude fosters a strong distrust and lack of respect between members of the two disciplines. If conversation with psychology is difficult for theologians with the other attitudes, for those with the xenophobic attitude, conversation is impossible.

Attitude and method are difficult to separate, but this INDEX model makes this valuable distinction possible.

A Practical Illustration of Integration*

The fact that Collins accorded a separate place to the professional in his wheel diagram of the areas of Practical Integration is noteworthy. Full-time psychological practitioners are especially interested in the implications of integration for the psychotherapeutic task. This is the place where "the rubber hits the road"; in other words, where the proof lies.

Since integration has been a theoretical endeavor by and large, it is with some relish that I propose a model for practical integration in the discussion that follows.

The state name ALaBaMa provides an acronym for the several facets of integrative psychotherapy that seem important. "A" represents the assumptions of faith. "L" represents the life predicament of the client(s) with whom one works in psychotherapy. "B" represents the background variables that provide the setting and relationship in which psychotherapy occurs. Finally, "M" represents the model of manipulation that one utilizes as a psychotherapeutic technique. These dimensions interact with each other in a cyclic, a dialogical, and a dialectical manner.

They interact cyclically in the sense that the therapist intentionally reflects on each of the dimensions in a repeated, ordered sequence with a given hour of psychotherapy. For example start with the assumptions of faith. In fact, I prepare myself daily by grounding myself in these assumptions through the reception of the Lord's Supper, Scripture reading, and prayer for those persons with whom I will work that day. I begin the hour by reminding myself silently of these assumptions and saying to myself something on the order of:

---

*These comments are a condensation of H. Newton Malony's "Psychotherapy: Where the Rubber Hits the Road," mimeographed, Fuller Theological Seminary, Pasadena, CA, 1978. Used with permission.

"This is a child of God with whom I am dealing—she/he is a sinner saved by grace who is seeking to find fulfillment and ministry—I am God's servant in this task—He is here with us."

Next, I become conscious of the life predicament of the person. I then return to a consciousness of the faith assumptions. Then, I reflect on the background situation in which we are working. In this phase I often note the time of day and my own feelings. Once more I return to the assumptions of faith in much the same manner that a backpacker refers to a compass. Then I concentrate on the model of manipulation I will use to guide the person in moving through his or her life predicament. I go through these dimensions in a cyclic fashion. The process could be diagrammed as follows:

Figure 12

Cyclic Interaction

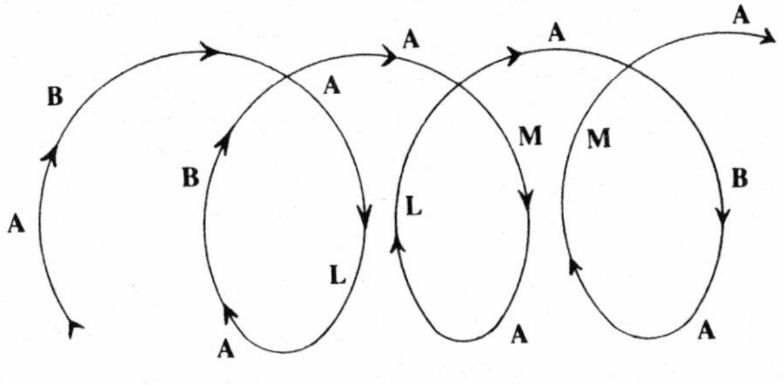

Furthermore, the "A," "L," "B," and "M" dimensions interact with each other in a *dialogical* manner. These elements of the situation "converse" with each other as the therapeutic hour progresses. It is an inner dialogue going on inside the therapist. I allow it and I intend it. Theodore Reik termed this process "listening with the third ear."

Whereas in the cyclic interaction the dimensions interact in a sequential manner in that one returns to the assumptions of faith in every other step; in the dialogic approach it is as if there were various dimensions, and they were seated around a conference table, engaged in a panel discussion. Which dimension will predominate at a given point in therapy is not predetermined. The dialogue progresses from moment to moment in an intuitive manner.

In Transactional Analysis terms, I stay as close to my Free Child as possible. I am confident, as was Berne, that there is within the child part of me an area of primitive intuition (often termed the Little Professor) that can be trusted. I implicitly count on this part of my own psyche to guide me in making judgments and in making interventions. I do not mean to imply that this part of me is uninformed or naïve. No, this Free Child listens to the conversation between the assumptions of faith, the life predicament, the background situation, and my methods of manipulation. I give power and a voice to each of these dimensions. They participate equally in the dialogue my Free Child hears. I simply mean there is a part of me that I try to leave free to make clinical judgments that are not couched in fancy words, theoretical logic, or my own prejudgments. I am brash enough to feel that this may be one of the ways God's Holy Spirit works in my life and in the lives of other Christian psychotherapists. This dialogical interaction could be diagrammed as in Figure 13.

I also suggested that the several dimensions of the Alabama theory of integrated psychotherapy interact with each other in a *dialectical* manner. The assumptions of faith, the life predicament, the background situation, and the methods of manipulation interpenetrate.

Simply put, in my reflections I consider the possibility that each of the dimensions could be understood in terms of the others and that any one of them could possibly be the very opposite of what it first appeared to be. To illustrate,

Figure 13

Dialogical Interaction

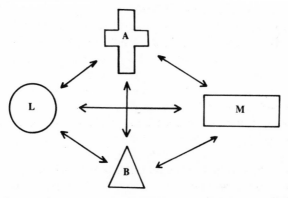

the issues of a person's life predicament may appear to be a matter of loneliness and neurotic dependency. However, understood in terms of the assumptions of faith, these symptoms may be indications of sinful self-preoccupation and a refusal to accept God's love. Again, background variables, such as the client's fee or my inner judgment about certain behaviors, may be more than attitudes. They may also be the signs of my own sinful weakness and lack of reliance on God's guidance. Furthermore, the assumptions of faith themselves may in part be reflections, prejudgments, and emphases of my own background.

In this interaction no one of the dimensions is held sacred. They are all considered to be fully understandable in terms of the other dimensions. For instance, the methods of manipulation are just that, but they are also assumptions of faith, and vice versa. Each of the dimensions influences and informs the others. These considerations allow me to probe the depths of meaning in my psychotherapeutic model. This healthy tension also prevents me from simplistically assuming that things are always what I say they are, or that I have a corner on the "really real." I, too, am a part of history and culture, with all their limitations. The client is not the only one caught in a life predicament. I am thus convinced of two things: first, irrespective of the different symptomology, both the client's situation and mine are states of basic anxiety that can be assuaged only through faith in a God who saves; and second, in spite of my good intentions, I serve a God who may need to forgive my best as well as my worst. This dialectical interaction could be diagrammed as follows.

Figure 14

Dialectical Interaction

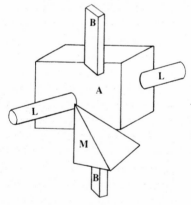

All three types of interaction among the dimensions (the assumptions of faith, the life predicament, the background situation, and the methods of manipulation) go on within the therapist's head. They are not communicated directly to the client, but they provide the foundation on which actual therapy occurs. *Cyclical* interaction refers to the sequential referral of all other dimensions back to assumptions of faith. *Dialogical* interaction refers to the conversation that goes on between the several dimensions and to which the Free Child in my psyche listens attentively. Finally, *dialectical* interaction refers to the interpenetration of all the dimensions in such a healthy tension that they are always more than they appear to be. Through these types of introspective reflections, the foundation is laid for truly integrative psychotherapy.

I turn next to a fuller description of the various dimensions in the Alabama model.

"A"—Assumptions of Faith

In discussing each dimension, I intend to delineate both its content and its genesis. In other words, I will detail what it is as well as how I come to know it.

These assumptions of faith are the fundamental presuppositions about the nature of persons, God, and the universe, which I bring to the psychotherapeutic task. I firmly agree with Collins that such assumptions are present in all psychologists' work. They may be implicit and unrecognized. They may be fleeing and changing, or persistent and permanent. But they are always there. I acknowledge and make my assumptions explicit. My intent is that these convictions will guide and inform whatever I do as a psychotherapist.

Initially, my faith is in a *God who acts*. For a Christian this is the key to all else. I accept the God of the Bible as *the* God. Thus, he is the God who created, who chose, who guided, who judged, who pleaded, who sent the Messiah, who redeemed. He is always moving toward, and in behalf of, his people. He is the God of history who makes his way known in and through time and space. His kingdom has come. His kingdom comes. His kingdom will come.

My faith also affirms that *persons are children of this God who acts*. They are made in his image and placed on earth to do his will and to participate with him in his creative, redemptive action. Persons forget and wilfully violate their heritage and their destiny. They become estranged from God and from their true selves. Nevertheless, they remain precious in the eyes of God.

I affirm that *the God who acts sent Jesus who redeems.* Out of the merciful and loving mind of God came the Messiah; who in life, in death, and in life beyond death, boldly declared "All of you are sinners, your fate is of your own making; but take courage, here is the good news; sins are forgiven; God is merciful; life is abundant and possible; you can begin again." These are the words of redemption. This is the work of Christ. God's man, Jesus, has come, and hope is abroad in the world!

Which leads me to my next affirmation, i.e., that *God is busy bringing his kingdom in.* Creation is not finished. We humans live between the times. We live after the time of his appearing in human flesh and before the time of his coming again. He will do his good work in history apart from us, yet through us. When the end time comes we will be surprised by joy. His power is greater than our efforts or our understanding. Nevertheless, he has deigned to use us in his kingdom-building and has called us brothers of Christ Jesus.

Therefore, I affirm the *universal call to discipleship.* We human beings have been put here for a purpose. This purpose has been the same since the time of Adam and Eve. We are here to have fellowship with God, to love one another, and to have dominion over the earth. No other type of life has the possibility of bringing contentment and fulfillment. All other types are violations of our essence. We were created to be disciples and to share the ministry of our Lord, Jesus Christ. This is true for all persons and at all times.

Finally, I affirm *the presence of the Holy Spirit.* This is integral to faith in a God who acts. He is present with us. He is here to inspire, to encourage, to sustain, and to guide us.

We are not alone. He is with us at all times and in all places. His will will be done—through us and through all persons. He is the agent of the God of Abraham, Isaac, Jacob, Jesus, Peter, and Paul. He is the Comforter. He will not let us forget who we are. He nurtures us in applying the mind of Christ to the events of every day.

Thus, these are the assumptions I make about God, persons, and the universe. They are part and parcel of the foundation on which I stand as a human being. They are me. I openly bring them to the task of psycotherapy, which I consider to be the ministry through which I express my discipleship.

Life Predicament

The "L" in my ALaBaMa model of integrative psychotherapy stands for the life predicament of those persons who come to me for help. Persons who seek my help are those who are having problems in living with courage and fulfillment. They are those who are not managing to deal effectively with the frustrations they experience with themselves, with others, and with the physical world as they work toward their life goals. They are those who are having difficulty dealing with the enigmas of life; i.e., tragedy, meaninglessness, and death.

The source for my understanding of this is the words they speak and the emotions they share. I not only hear, but also understand; because I, too, am a person who knows what it is to face life's enigmas and to experience frustration. Their story has authority for me because I am also a human being.

I also understand people's life predicaments in terms of the model suggested by the Christian existentialist theologian Paul Tillich (1951), who suggested that this was the age of anxiety. All people, according to this model, experience two types of anxiety. On the one hand, they experience horizontal, or neurotic, anxiety. This is the insecurity they feel in relation to other human beings and to the world around them. They do not feel accepted or effective in getting and receiving love or in making their existence comfortable or secure. On the other hand, persons experience vertical or basic anxiety. This is the insecurity people experience when they come up against the "boundary situations" of life, as the psychiatrist Karl Jaspers called them. These are anxieties about meaninglessness and about guilt. Meaninglessness refers to conclusions about the evil and tragic and to the sense that one's life has no purpose. Guilt refers to the awareness that there is within oneself a proclivity for selfishness and aggression that leads to a profound need for forgiveness. Despair is probably a better word than anxiety for these basic concerns.

Taking this analysis one step further, I sense that much neurotic anxiety is grounded in basic anxiety. As Tillich suggests the answers to basic anxiety ultimately must come from outside the situation, i.e., from outside interpersonal relations and beyond any effort to master this physical world. No amount of rearranging the ways persons relate to each other and no amount of success in achievement will suffice to quiet these basic anxieties about meaninglessness and about guilt. The answer must come from beyond. Thus, in analyzing of the life predicament, I lay the groundwork for the reception of a solution that comes out of the assumptions of faith.

Background Variables

The "B" in the ALaBaMa model stands for the background variables, or the context in which psychotherapy takes place. The context includes other things on the therapist's mind, the time of the day, ulterior motives in both the client and in myself, world affairs, and unexpected life events.

Everything that is happening in the world is possibly a part of the environment of psychotherapy. Of course, considering all the background would be impossible and unmanageable. The job of the therapist is to assess the significant context of psychotherapy and keep it in mind as they work together. Nothing occurs in a vacuum. The sharing, the insights, the experiences, and the changes that comprise the content of therapy—all go on in context. I must consider all the elements that make up that context for the person and myself.

The interventions I attempt and the wisdom I share never come "from out of the blue." They emerge from the context. Nor are they ever received by a mind devoid of all thoughts except those the therapist puts there. I can only be partially aware of my client's environment. However, it is my job to be aware as much as possible of the environment's influence on any problem.

Model of Manipulation

The "M" in the model stands for my model of manipulation. This is another term for my preferred psychotherapeutic system. Active manipulation is not a bad technique for a legitimate behavioral scientist. Intervention techniques are inherent to any good theory of psychotherapy. They reflect the social scientific concern for planned change. They are a counter to wishful thinking that people will grow on their own. I consider myself to be solidly identified with those scientist-professionals who come to the psychotherapeutic situation with a plan in mind. I judge as inadequate the lazy thinking that affirms that "people will get better if you just give them somebody to talk to."

It is just such errant thinking as this that makes sense out of the Carkhuff (1968) research Collins quoted. I would judge that the lack of reported differences in the lay and professional counselors was observed in a group of practitioners who set the therapeutic conditions of "empathy, congruence, and warmth," and then waited for something to happen. Therapeutic conditions are not enough; the psychotherapist must actively intervene. It is no wonder that no difference was noted between trained and untrained persons. The ability to provide therapeutic conditions is quite likely more art than training. It is probably at least as dependent on the skill of the therapist as on the training he or she has received. Something more than therapeutic conditions was needed.

It is the "something more" that separates counselors from psychotherapists. Counselors set up the conditions and then wait for something to happen. Psychotherapists also set up the conditions, but then make things happen by applying their model of manipulation. I have strong doubts that the Carkhuff research could be replicated among the skilled psychotherapists with whom I am acquainted.

This leads me to a very brief statement about my own model of manipulation, which is Transactional Analysis. I intentionally structure my understanding of each client's problem by this model and apply techniques to restructure the person's interactive style in TA terms. I avoid the eclectic approach to psychotherapy, which is that every client is unique, and one applies whatever psychotherapeutic technique one thinks is appropriate. The eclectic therapist usually does not know what is happening and neither does the client. If anything good comes from such a relationship, it is quite by accident. I inform persons when they initially come for help that I use Transactional Analysis, a theory that places heavy emphasis on healthy interpersonal relating.

The Goals of Psychotherapy

The goal of the Alabama theory of integrated psychotherapy is "healing that leads to holiness." This unites the twin goals of adjustment and fulfillment. Furthermore, healing and holiness resolve both neurotic and basic anxiety problems referred to earlier.

"Healing" means returning to a state of well-being. In the negative sense, it is freedom from sickness. In the positive sense, it is an ability to function or a state of robustness. It pertains to a balance in which one is not experiencing the symptoms of illness. When people say, "I'm O.K., things are going pretty well, I'm managing, haven't felt bad in a long time," they are defining health as absence of illness. On the other hand, health can mean achieving a goal or reaching an ideal. When people say, "You should see me, I can run three miles, my blood pressure is down, I'm no longer bothered by fears—I can even talk to strangers, I'm really feeling strong," they are defining health as the ability to function.

I am interested in both definitions of health and take each of them as a goal. Often the negative state of health precedes the positive. Being afraid of high places or having fantasies that one is being looked at must stop before one feels free to go anywhere without fear, or is able to spend hours in a public library reading without looking up to see if anyone is watching. I am seldom satisfied simply with the disappearance of a symptom, but want to assist the person in additional progress, leading to a significantly increased ability to live with pride and courage. The goal is better adjustment. It is also self-fulfillment.

Health is not only self-fulfillment, but wholeness. Being "whole" means being unified, integrated, or complete. Gestalt psychologists, with their dictum, "Lose your mind and come to your senses," are using this definition of health in their effort to unite cognition with emotion. They assume that most people are cut off from their emotions and thus are sick.

Another more pertinent aspect pertains to the spiritual part of persons. Instead of being cut off from their emotions, people are often separated from the spiritual part of themselves. In biblical terms, persons were made in the image of God, and through their sin they have lost contact with their true natures. Thus, they are sick or estranged. Returning to spiritual health means becoming reunited with the image of God or the nature in which they were originally created. As long as persons remain separated from this part of themselves they are sick. Deep within the individual is the sense of who he or she really is, i.e., a child of God. The individual knows this, but acts as if he were ignorant. In psychotherapy, one of my goals is to make my clients whole again by helping them become reunited with their true natures. I am confident that this is possible because, as Tillich reportedly said "when man and God meet it is the reuniting of the estranged, not the meeting of the strange." By becoming whole in this way, persons return to their true natures and so are healthy again.

This healing leads directly to the second goal of therapy, i.e., holiness. I indicated that my goals were "health that leads to holiness." Holiness refers to being set apart for, or belonging to, God. Holiness is a state or way of behaving that indicates one is living up to an ideal or trying to be a genuinely pious or religious person. Holiness indicates a person has found the meaning of life in a relationship with God. Holiness is a quality of those who are dependent on God and look to him for guidance.

Obviously, when holiness is stated as a goal of therapy, the integrative nature of psychotherapy becomes clear. I believe that psychotherapy is not complete until a person turns from resolving the problems of living to making a forthright attempt to live life in terms of faith. This is sound psychology if, as I believe, real life is life that is lived in terms of purpose or meaning, regardless of whether that meaning is religious. Viktor Frankl, in his espousal of logotherapy, agrees with this position. The late Gordon Allport suggested that life was best lived in terms of being pulled into the future by some value rather than being pushed by the habits of the past—no matter how good those habits might be. This is also sound theology, affirming what St. Augustine said in his well-known prayer, "our hearts are restless till they find their rest in thee." Abundant life is that which is lived in response to, and dependence upon, God as he is revealed in Jesus Christ our Lord.

Holiness, therefore, refers to a quality of life wherein persons acknowledge that they are children of God and confess their errors in trying to build life on any other basis. Furthermore, it includes a willingness to be a disciple, i.e., live life in dependence on the grace, acceptance, love, and power of God, rather than on the basis of one's own strength. Finally, it includes an intention to discover one's God-given gift and a commitment to use that gift in ministry to others. In the words of John Wesley, holiness means setting one's goal to "go on to perfection in this life."

My intent is to be as explicit about these goals as I am about my assumption of faith and my model of manipulation. I present this paradigm as a practical plan of integration that works in psychotherapy. It is an illustration of an intentional process that I feel is essential for all would-be integrators.

Summary

This response has attempted to deal with four basic addenda to Collins' presentation. The discussion pertained to the issues of the socio-cultural dimensions of integration, the nature of contemporary society, which is the context of integration, a model for understanding integrative attitudes, and a practical paradigm for integrative psychotherapy.

As noted in the beginning, these are adjoiners in the sense that they are near enough to touch Collins' ideas, but they add to those ideas dimensions that appear to be important to include.

CHAPTER 5

Integration: The Advances

Gary R. Collins

Several years ago, during a conversation with Paul Tournier, I asked how this well-known author responded to reviews of his books.

"I always learn from them," Tournier replied. "I enjoy reading them because they are helpful to me in my work."

But I pressed the old doctor farther. "How do you react if the reviews are critical of your work?

The reply was revealing. "When criticized, I am grateful for reviewers who have taken time to read my books and give their reactions, even when these reactions strongly disagree with what I have written."

Periodically I think of Tournier's remarks whenever I read critiques such as the previous chapter. Those who respond to my work are sometimes critical and not hesitant to take positions with which I disagree. But respondents such as Dr. Malony pay me a warm compliment in looking at my work seriously enough to point out strengths and weaknesses. I am deeply grateful for such thoughtful reactions and for the kindness and clarity with which these so often are expressed. In this concluding chapter I would like to respond to some of the critiques of my work, raise some questions about integration, and make some observations about integration in the future.

Some Responses to Criticism

The first three chapters of this book were originally presented as a series of lectures. These were followed by stimulating interaction with a number of students, psychologists, and other scholars. At Fuller Theological Seminary, there even was a class that had the assignment of preparing written critiques of my lectures. Reading them was a sobering and humbling experience.

Consider, for example, the creative student who began her critique with the following introduction:

> Psychologists! Tired of being pushed around by psychoanalysts and Sunday school teachers? Do sidewalk evangelists kick sand in your face? Do psychiatrists treat you as an illusion? Now there is an amazing new product for you: IOPAT (Integration-of-Psychology-and-Theology). IOPAT can relieve your tensions at the lab, on the couch, and in your local church. IOPAT enables you to communicate with Freudians and Fundamentalists alike! (Behaviorists extra). ORDER YOUR INTRODUCTORY SAMPLE NOW!
>
> Over the years I've ordered many of these, in various sizes and models: Humanistic-existentialist (Havens, 1968), polemical (Mowrer, 1969), and pacifist (Tournier, 1965; Jeeves, 1976). But when the goods are delivered, what I receive seems to be only a more elaborate advertisement, not a working model. In fact, I've never even gotten a blueprint, so that I could build one myself.
>
> I'm afraid I have the same reaction to the current Collins model. In this case, the advertisement is beautifully written, and the claims of the product are elaborated in more detail than usual. A glowing description is given of the

many settings in which it may be used: professional, pastoral, peer, apologetic, public, and preventive. Its superiority to earlier versions is explained in some detail. There are even general specifications included, with major components listed. But there is no description of the tolerances or operating characteristics of these components. There are no schematic diagrams. There is no fully operational model in the package.

I'm beginning to suspect, however, that I might not know how to recognize an "integration" if I saw one. Collins does not bother to define the term for us, except by demonstrating previous denotations. I confess that I am not sure what the "integration of psychology and theology" implies for him. Does it mean open dialogue between psychology and theology? An end to sniping and name-calling? Use of the same linguistic categories and methods? Asking the same questions? Reaching the same conclusions? Collins does not clearly define which brand of psychology and theology he wants to integrate (Doran, 1978).[11]

The writer of these paragraphs has identified an issue which I have heard often: the problem of language and nomenclature. What is psychology? What do we mean by theology? Do psychologists really understand theological language, and do theologians understand psychological terms? In the future, the diversity of psychologies and theologies must be acknowledged, and our terminology must be defined in such a way that understanding is enhanced.

In all this, however, we must be careful not to spend so much time trying to define terms that we never proceed beyond this linguistic issue. It is possible to get bogged down in endless debates over teminology and never move to consider such important and practical integration

---

[11]From Constance Doran, unpublished response to the Finch Lectures, Fuller Theological Seminary, 1978. Used with permission.

questions as the role of the Bible, the place of theology, and the influence of culture.

The Bible and Integration

Several recent writers have suggested, correctly I believe, that psychology has become the contemporary religion in our culture. For some people, the psychologist is the new priest, with a cultic vocabulary, holy books and sacraments. He or she absolves the guilty, sets guidelines for marriage and family, comforts the lonely, keeps vigil with the dying, and calls the flock to honesty, integrity, and openness. This is a sobering observation, which has been elaborated with even greater clarity in the book by Paul Vitz (1977), which was mentioned in the previous chapter.

According to Vitz, psychology as a religion exists in great strength throughout the United States. As a religion, psychology is deeply anti-Christian and hostile to most other religions. Nevertheless, "psychology as religion is extensively supported by schools, universities, and social programs financed by taxes collected from millions of Christians. This use of tax money to support what has become a secular state religion raises grave political and legal issues." The author goes on to argue that "psychology as religion has for years been destroying individuals, families, and communities," and has become a form of "secular humanism based on worship of the self" (Vitz, 1977, p. 10).

If such a view is correct (and Vitz makes his case persuasively), then psychology has already become a major challenge to historical Christianity. Little wonder that some Christians have vehemently opposed psychology and argued that the science of human behavior is both unnecessary and harmful to Christianity.

Christians within the field usually do not accept this conclusion. We see the value of psychology, but we also can see its dangers. I, for one, believe that psychology has great but restricted potential. It can be helpful and of immense practical value, but it cannot become our national religion. It must be secondary to the teaching of Christianity as found in the Bible.

There are differences, however, in our views concerning the extent to which psychology should be "brought under the authority of Scripture." While I surely respect those who think otherwise, I am firmly committed to the position that the Bible must be our ultimate source of truth and that conclusions from psychology must be tested against the teachings of Scripture—as we understand these, using the best hermeneutics possible.

Such a statement leads to one's view of the authority of the Bible. In attempting to summarize my position, Arthur Glasser has written that

> to Collins, the Bible represents God's authority, and is like God—outside the flow of history. Its propositions and texts are not culturally conditioned. . . . The Bible is a collection of sentences—each one with the label 'TRUTH' and each proposition a self-contained, infallible revelation. The Word of God is reduced to Bible texts a fallible person can infallibly use. This Word is a complex set of rules for our faith and conduct, admittedly given to the Israelites (in the Old Testament) and to certain sections of the Apostolic Church (in the New Testament) but which are not related to any existing culture today.*

I would suggest that this is a stereotype that has been imposed on me and is not an accurate reflection of the position I took in the first three chapters of this book. Perhaps Glasser confuses that which is culturally expressed with that which is culturally bound. I would agree that the biblical truths were revealed or expressed culturally. It

---

*From Arthur F. Glasser's "Integration Is Impossible If God Speaks with Two Voices", mimeographed, Fuller Theological Seminary, Pasadena, California, 1978. Quoted with permission.

does not follow, however, that the Bible is then culturally bound in a way that limits its relevance for us today.

The above quote also loses sight of the fact that biblical interpretation must always take place within historical and textual context. Very few people, in my opinion, would agree that sentences should be lifted out of the Bible and interpreted as "self-contained, infallible revelation" completely apart from the context in which they were expressed.

Dr. Glasser also asserts that "Collins assumes, of course, that there is no problem involved in calling forth the witness of any Bible text. Fallible though he is, he can nonetheless use Scripture so infallibly that its witness is not diminished in the least. . . . Since, at best, we are terribly flawed by the Fall, we desperately need the illumination of the Holy Spirit to guide us as we become involved in this exegesis and translation." I agree with this last sentence, but it is not true that I see "no problem involved in calling forth the witness of any Bible text" or that I claim to interpret the Scripture infallibly. Hermeneutics is both a difficult and important field. Certainly, no one person has an infallible understanding or application of Scripture.

I am in agreement with the student who wrote that "psychologists who are trained in, and committed to, an objective, systematic method of investigation will often abandon the stance when dealing with the investigation of the data of Scripture. They, then, often open Pandora's box of subjectivism, unacknowledged bias, inconsistent methodology, and selective use of data—none of which they would condone as a scientist. To avoid committing the above errors the integrator must become, not merely acquainted with, but expert in, hermeneutics" (Bixler, 1978). To understand and apply good principles of hermeneutics does not insure that we will reach infallible interpretations, but it does keep us from error that slips in so easily when we fail to interpret the Scriptures with good hermeneutical principles.

In the preceding chapter, Malony writes that "the Bible . . . does not seek to convey its authority by texts. Texts are but empirical data, and Christians are called to experience 'true' truth through encounter with God. Only through establishing existential touch with Jesus as he is disclosed in the Bible does the Christian begin to enter into the Bible's authority." To me this sounds like a popular theological view that sees revelation located in events and experiences, but not in words of the Bible. Such a view elevates personal experience above biblical authority—a procedure that has characterized much pastoral counseling in the past.

In a perceptive comment on this issue, Thomas Oden has written that, in pastoral care, the

> overwhelming weight of authority for theological knowledge is given to experience, and in this sense the American pastoral care movement belongs essentially to the tradition of a liberalizing, pragmatizing, pietism. One first does certain things and experiences certain relationships, like shepherding the flock, and only then draws valid theological conclusions. . . . Although we hardly wish to challenge the validity of interview analysis in pastoral care, we seriously question whether this alone is adequate as a vantage point for drawing theological conclusions without the theological equilibrium that comes from the sustained study of Scripture and tradition and the struggle for rational and systematic self consistency (1967, pp. 89, 90).[12]

Such a sustained study of the Scripture must look to what the Scriptures say verbally rather than "establishing existential touch with Jesus." Scripture must be interpreted correctly in the integration process, but clearly there is disagreement on what correct interpretation means.

---

[12]From Thomas C. Oden, *Contemporary Theology and Psychotherapy* (Philadelphia: Westminster Press, 1967), by permission of the author.

Theology and Integration

Is it possible for one to work on the integration of psychology and theology but ignore contemporary theology? According to one reviewer, I have tended to "remain within the narrow confines of evangelicalism and seem unaware of literature that has emerged in the past 50 years among mainline Protestants on the complex relationship between psychology and theology" (Rambo, 1977). This is a good warning, although I try to keep aware of the body of theological literature and agree that any complete discussion of integration must take theological diversity into consideration. In my writings, however, I have chosen to restrict myself to psychology and *evangelical* theologies. This in no way implies that nothing has been done by others who have been writing in this field since the days of Anton Boisen and before.

Of greater interest to me in the area of theology is the suggestion that my work serves to draw psychology completely into the theological enterprise. To remove psychology from the community of the social sciences and into the camp of theology would be of no advantage for either side. I have no desire to see psychology swallowed up by theology (for one thing, this would put me out of a job), but I think psychology must recognize the philosophical and theological foundations on which it is built. In like manner theology must acknowledge the psychological dimensions and implications of its discipline. Malony is correct in stating that it is not easy to stand on the border between two fields, but if some people do not do so there is a danger of psychology's slipping subtly into philosophy and theology,* or of theology's becoming no more than a psychological system.

---

*Surely Skinner moved out of science and into philosophy-theology when he wrote *Walden Two* (1948). Selye's *Stress Without Distress* (1974) reflects a similar move.

The integrator must have good familiarity with both theology and psychology. For too long, integration has been the interest of psychologists but not of theologians. When a psychologist who lacks biblical and theological education tries to integrate psychology and theology, he or she will run into the same simplicities and over-generalizations that we have seen recently in the writings and seminar conclusions of some evangelical pastors who clearly do not really understand what is happening in the social sciences. Ideally the task of integration must be carried out by persons with dual competence. Even better, perhaps, would be integration carried out by teams of social scientists and theologians who respect each other and who share an interest in understanding human behavior, helping people change and bringing the insights of psychology into the service of the church.

Culture and Integration

Over the years, it has been my privilege to travel to a number of foreign countries, and in so doing I have learned to appreciate cultural differences. I have tried to refllect such differences in my writing and in any speeches I have been invited to give to foreign audiences.

I am, therefore, somewhat chagrined by but largely in agreement with, the observation that I have ignored cultural differences in my views of integration. Of course it is true that human beings work within a socio-cultural, ethno-psychological context. Many years ago Freud forgot that human behavior is culturally stamped and reached some conclusions that were strongly condemned by Malinowski and others who were more alert to cultural differences. In the past I have been critical of psychologists and psychological popularizers who have attempted to present "universal" psychological laws and "biblical principles" that are much more culture bound than the speaker realizes or would advocate. I must not make a similar error.

Had a sociologist read the first three chapters of this book, he or she perhaps might have responded as did three speakers at a recent psychology convention. In describing *The Rebuilding of Psychology* (Collins, 1977) they wrote:

> Collins does make reference to the social dimension of human experience. . . . The picture we are given is that of the autonomous individual influenced by an external society. We would suggest that the society . . . is more than influence. . . . Individual and society are inextricably interwoven. . . .
>
> Not only does Collins neglect to give the social dimension of existence sufficient emphasis, there is also a blatant lack of evaluation of the society in which we live. When social problems are ignored as being peripheral to the real problems of man, such as alienation, personal insecurity, being and becoming, etc., attention is not given to the impact of a dehumanizing massified society which is directly responsible for the repression of humanity. Lack of a systematic social critique results in the passive acceptance of the prevailing ideology. Collins purports to be a critic of the dehumanization of man, but his lack of social analysis beyond the individual places him in the precarious position of accepting the very social reality which promotes the dehumanization of man (Dueck, et al., 1978, p. 7, 8).[13]

These are strong words that I don't particularly like to read, but they have considerable validity, and in the future I would hope to be more sensitive to the cultural and social aspects both of integration and of the psychological tasks of understanding human behavior or helping people change.

---

[13]From A. Dueck, K. Genich, and P. Higgins, "Models of integration: A critique of Jeeves and Collins," Paper presented at the Convention of the Christian Association for Psychological Studies, Chicago, April 14, 1978. Used by permission.

Some Questions About Integration

The integration of psychology and theology is a growing field, especially among evangelicals. The INDEX approach summarized in Figure 11 (p. 102) is a creative attempt to organize some present integration efforts. As work in this area continues, however, several basic quetions must be answered.

Who should integrate? It has been suggested that the best integration will be done by the trained pyschologists who is also a committed Christian and discerning theologian. Such a psychologist needs enough biblical and theological insight to ask the right questions, and he or she needs the honesty and commitment to face the implications of the answers. When this is not possible, the integrator must have at least a good knowledge of psychology and theology, and must be committed to integration, not only as an intellectual exercise, but as a part of his or her life. To a Christian, helping people grow psychologically and spiritually is too important a task to be taken lightly or relegated to ivory-tower discussion.

Is integration theoretical or practical? In the preceding paragraphs I have made little reference to Malony's ALaBaMa approach, not because this was unappreciated (indeed he said many significant things), but because it was more a statement of his theory of psychotherapy than it was a commentay on the integration of psychology and theology. Surely it is true that integration is more than an intellectual exercise. The practical relating of the Christian faith with the skillful application of psychotherapeutic techniques is basic to integration.

I wonder, however, if we can really contrast counselors and psychotherapists. According to Malony, "counselors set up the conditions and then wait for something to happen. Psychotherapists also set up the conditions, but then make things happen by applying their model of manipulation." I doubt that many professionals would agree with this distinction. Numerous counselors, including lay counselors who have a minimum of training, have a model of manipulation that they apply, often to the benefit (and sometimes to the detriment) of the counselee. I am uncomfortable about the idea of elevating such psychotherapy to the kind of high and mighty level that puts it above and beyond counseling. This is an artificial distinction that sounds good in theory, but is difficult to support in practice.

Who cares about integration? It has been suggested that Christianity exists in a secular milieu that has little need for, or interest in, Christian theology. Christian psychologists have a strong interest in integration and can appreciate the importance of a Christian philosophical foundation for their work. The secular world does not see this, however, and often fails to appreciate its own philosophical foundations.

In the future, integration will continue to be of concern primarily to Christian psychologists. The nonbeliever, if he or she has any interest in this subject, is likely to be interested in psychological explanations for religious behavior, values, and beliefs. This in itself is a worthy subject for study, but there will always be psychologists (including Christian psychologists) who cannot see the importance of studying the integration issue. More attention needs to be directed to demonstrating why integration is important and needed.

*What are we integrating?** At some time in the integration process, each of us must ask What are we integrating? Theology and psychology are complex fields, each filled with complex assumptions, changing data, and issues that bring heated debate. Neither field is unified or static. This, of course, makes our task more difficult and has led some to question whether integration is possible (see Carter and Narramore, 1979) or even desirable.

---

*The remainder of this chapter is adapted with permission from Collins (1980).

Pascoe (1980) deals with this complexity by considering the "philosphical underpinnings" of psychology and attempting to construct "a Christian world view which will provide a frame of reference for the integration of psychological and Christian thought." In this respect, Pascoe's work is similar to that of Collins (1977), Sutherland and Poelstra (1979), Myers (1978), Cosgrove (1979), Larzelere (1980), and Wertheimer (1972). Wertheimer's volume could be read with great profit by any serious student of integration. These works raise at least three important considerations for integrators.

First, there is the reality of blind spots. Both psychology and theology have them, and so do those of us who work in these and related disciplines. Special care must be taken in our study of biblical data. When we accept the Bible as the true Word of God, we sometimes assume that our interpretations are equally infallible. Kraft (1970) addresses this succinctly. We must recognize, he writes, "the man-madeness and fallibility of every academic discipline. There is no essential superiority of 'The Queen of the Sciences' (theology) over any other discipline, even though we may contend that the scriptural data that theologians work with is more sacred than data ordinarily treated by other disciplines" (p. 170). The psychological conclusions about selective perception (and selective inattention) apply to most, if not all, of us in the integration filed.

Second, there is a need for continued work in apologetics. It is widely agreed that attention must be given to our foundational presuppositions, but why do we accept the assumptions that we do? Are not some beginning points more valid (logical and probable) than others? Why, for example, should we integrate psychology with the Bible's view of reality? Why should one accept a supernatural orientation or the reality of Christ?

It can be argued that apologetics is the work of specialists other than psychologists. Social scientists do not claim to be experts in apologetics, so we must build on the work of others. Surely, however, the integrator must at least be familiar with the reasons for Christian beliefs.

Freud, Ellis, Skinner, and a host of others have attacked Christianity on psychological grounds. Rarely, it seems, have their attacks been answered systematically with psychological soundness and theological-apologetic awareness. Little has been done to provide a solid rationale for our presuppositions and our epistemology. In the field of integration, perhaps we need a "psychological apologetic" that is biblically based and alert to psychological data and criticisms. Such work could help greatly in integration.

Finally, we need to give continued consideration to the issue of practical relevance. How often do we reach the end of scholarly papers with a disturbing thought: this is stimulating and interesting to read, but so what? Does it have any practical value?

The issue of "pure" versus "applied" science has been debated for decades, perhaps for centuries, and it is not likely to be solved now. I would suggest, however, that Christians always must have some concern for the practical. Jesus debated religious leaders, stated theological truths, and demonstrated his intellectual capacities, but he constantly ministered to the needy, and his life and work had a strong practical orientation. The integration of psychology and theology can be a stimulating intellectual exercise, but ultimately our integration efforts must improve our ability to help others and to minister to their needs.

Some Suggestions for the Future

In their recent volume, Carter and Narramore (1979) have emphasized that we still have far to go in our integration work. They have written that:

nearly all past efforts at the integration of psychology and theology suffer from one or more of the following deficiencies:

1. They tend to be piecemeal or based on proof-texted approaches to the problem of integration and, consequently, lack comprehensiveness.
2. They are lacking in either psychological or theological sophistication or both.
3. They attempt to press the data of Scripture onto psychology, or vice versa, in a way that is inappropriate and does not do justice to both disciplines.
4. They lack a well-defined view of the nature of the human being.
5. They lack clearly defined theological and philosophical underpinnings.
6. They lack objective scientific data.
7. They lack a well-thought-out theory of personality.
8. They lack a theory of counseling that issues out of a comprehensive view of the human being and maladjustment.

These weaknesses have resulted in a dearth of writings that are biblically consistent, psychologically "accurate", and meaningfully integrated at both the conceptual and practical levels. Until these weaknesses are overcome, it will be impossible to have a systematic and comprehensive Christian view of psychology. And it will be impossible to integrate the data of psychology and Scripture in a way that significantly benefits both disciplines (p. 30).[14]

The eight deficiencies identified in the above quotation can also be a formula for future work. We must work to remove these deficiencies. In addition, we must recognize that there may be different levels of integration; different

---

[14]From *The Integration of Psychology and Theology: An Introduction*, by John A. Carter and Bruce Narramore, copyright © 1979 by The Zondervan Corporation. Used by permission.

theories, conclusions, and personal approaches; different assumptions; and different methods in our practical integration work. I suggest that there also must be a recognition of the value of input from disciplines such as sociology, anthropology, biology, and philosophy. Evangelical integrators cannot ignore developments in pastoral counseling and the field of pastoral psychology. We must be alert to developing issues in the psychology of religion, the examination of religious experience, and the scientific study of religion.

Clearly, the integration of psychology and theology cannot be a one-person enterprise. There will continue to be different areas of emphasis and different centers of study. In the decades ahead, we surely must develop additional centers for training people in a field that is in its infancy, but is showing signs of rapid growth. If the present is any indication of the future, it is likely that the state of the art of integration will be more difficult to analyze in 1990 and 2000 because of its continuing expansion. Perhaps we even are on the threshold of the development of a new discipline that has great relevance for the future.

At the beginning of this book, I described my first encounters with psychology and theology—as a freshman required to spend weekly sessions visiting a state hospital. Some of the questions that concerned me in those early days still persist, unanswered. But today, many capable people are working on integration issues and progress is already becoming apparent. To me this is both encouraging and exciting.

References

Adams, J. *The Christian Counselor's Manual.* Grand Rapids: Baker Book House, 1973.

———. *Competent to Counsel.* Grand Rapids: Baker Book House, 1970.

Allport, G. W. *The Individual and His Religion.* New York: The Macmillan Co., 1950.

Barber, C. J., Colwell, W. E., and Strauss, G. H. "Psychological wholeness and the needs of man." *Journal of Psychology and Theology, 4,* 1975, pp. 258-67.

Bube, R. H. *The Human Quest: A New Look at Science and Christian Faith.* Waco, TX: Word Books, 1971.

Bixler, W. "The role of hermeneutics in the integration of psychology and theology." Unpublished paper. Fuller Theological Seminary, Pasadena, CA, 1978.

Caplan, G. *Principles of Preventive Psychiatry.* New York: Basic Books, 1964.

Carkhuff, R. R. *Helping and Human Relations: Vol. I and II.* New York: Holt, Rinehart & Winston, 1969.

———. "Differential functioning of lay and professional helpers." *Journal of Counseling Psychology,* 15, 1968, 117-28.

Carnell, E. J. *An Introduction of Christian Apologetics.* Grand Rapids: Eerdmans Publishing Co., 1948.

Carter, J. D. "Secular and sacred models of psychology and religion." *Journal of Psychology and Theology, 5,* Summer 1977, pp. 197-208.

Carter, J. D. and Mohline, R. J. *Journal of Psychology and Theology, 4,* 1976, pp. 3-14.

Carter, J. D. and Narramore, B. *The Integration of Psychology and Theology: An Introduction.* Grand Rapids: Zondervan Publishing House, 1979.

Clinebell, H. J., Jr. *The Mental Health Ministry of the Local Church.* New York: Abingdon Press, 1965.

———. *Basic Types of Pastoral Counseling:* Nashville: Abingdon Press, 1966.

Collins, G. R. *Effective Counseling.* Carol Stream: Creation House, 1972.

———. *The Christian Psychology of Paul Tournier.* Grand Rapids: Baker Book House, 1973.

———. *How to Be a People Helper.* Santa Ana, CA: Vision House, 1976*a.*

———. *People Helper Growthbook.* Santa Ana, CA: Vision House, 1976*b.*

———. *The Rebuilding of Psychology: An Integration of Psychology and Christianity.* Wheaton: Tyndale, 1977.

———. "Integrating psychology and theology: Some reflections on the state of the art." *Journal of Psychology and Theology, 8,* 1980, pp. 72-9.

Cox, H. "Eastern cults and western culture. Why young Americans are buying Oriental religion." *Psychology Today, 11,* July 1977, pp. 36-42.

Crabb, L. J., Jr. *Basic Principles of Biblical Counseling.* Grand Rapids: Zondervan Publishing House, 1975.

—————. *Effective Biblical Counseling*. Grand Rapids: Zondervan Publishing House, 1977.

Crane, W. E. *Where God Comes In: The Divine "Plus" in Counseling*. Waco, TX: Word Books, 1970.

Danish, S. J. *Helping Skills: A Basic Training Program*. New York: Behavioral Publications, 1973.

Doran, C. Response to the Finch Lectures. Unpublished paper. Fuller Theological Seminary, Pasadena, CA, 1978.

Drakeford, J. W. *Counseling for Church Leaders*. Nashville: Broadman Press, 1961.

—————. *Integrity Therapy*. Nashville: Broadman Press, 1967.

Dueck, A., Genich, K. and Higgins, P. "Models of integration: A critique of Jeeves and Collins." Paper presented at Convention of Christian Association for Psychological Studies, Chicago, April 14, 1978.

Egan, G. *The Skilled Helper: A Model for Systematic Helping and Interpersonal Relating*. Monterey, CA: Brooks/Cole, 1975.

Farnsworth, K. E. "Embodied integration." *Journal of Psychology and Theology, 2*, 1974, pp. 116-24.

—————. "Models for the integration of psychology and theology." Paper presented at the Annual Meeting of the American Scientific Affiliation, Wheaton College, Wheaton, Illinois, August 20-23, 1976.

Frankl, V. E. *The Unconscious God*. New York: Simon & Schuster, 1975.

Freud, S. *The Future of an Illusion*. Garden City, NY: Doubleday & Co., 1927.

—————. *Moses and Monotheism*. New York: Random House, 1939.

—————. *Totem and Taboo*. London: Routledge & Kegan Paul, 1913.

————. "A religious experience" (1928). In *Collected Papers, 5,* New York: Basic Books, 1959, pp. 243-46.

Fromm, E. *Man for Himself.* New York: Holt, Rinehart, & Winston, 1947.

————. *Psychoanalysis and Religion.* New York: Bantam Books, 1950.

————. *You Shall Be As Gods: A Radical Interpretation of the Old Testament and Its Tradition.* New York: Holt, Rinehart & Winston, 1966.

Gartner, A. and Riessman, F. *Self Help in the Human Services.* San Francisco: Jossey-Bass, 1977.

Gilkey, L. *Naming the Whirlwind: The Renewal of God-language.* Indianapolis: Bobbs-Merrill, 1969.

Glasser, A. "Integration is impossible if God speaks with two voices." Mimeographed, Fuller Theological Seminary, Pasadena, CA, 1978.

Greeley, A. M. "Popular psychology and the gospel." *Theology Today, 33,* 1976, pp. 224-31.

Havens, J. *Psychology and Religion: A Contemporary Dialogue.* Princeton, NJ: Van Nostrand Reinhold Co., 1968.

Havens, J. "The participant's vs. the observer's frame of reference in the psychological study of religion." In H. N. Malony (ed.) *Current Perspectives in the Psychology of Religion.* Grand Rapids: Eerdmans, 1977, pp. 101-5. (Reprinted from the *Journal for the Scientific Study of Religion, 1,* 1961.)

Henninger, D. "Self-Help Books as Spiritual Counselors." *Wall Street Journal,* 1977.

Hiltner, S. *The Counselor in Counseling.* New York: Abingdon Press, 1950.

————. *Preface to Pastoral Theology.* Nashville: Abingdon Press, 1958.

Homans, P. Introduction in P. Homans (ed.), *The*

Dialogue Between Theology and Psychology. The University of Chicago Press, 1968, pp. 1-10.

Howe, R. *The Miracle of Dialogue.* New York: The Seabury Press, 1963.

Jeeves, M. A. *Psychology and Christianity: The View Both Ways.* Downers Grove, IL: InterVarsity, 1976.

Joint Commission on Mental Illness and Health. *Action for Mental Health.* New York: Science Editions, 1961.

Jung, C. G. *Psychology and Religion.* New Haven: Yale University Press, 1938.

Katz, A. H. and Bener, E. I. (eds.) *The Strength In Us: Self Help Groups in the Modern World.* New York: New Viewpoints, 1976.

Kraft, C. "Can anthropological insight assist evangelical theology?" *Christian Scholars' Review, 7,* 1977, pp. 165-202.

La Haye, T. *How to Win Over Depression.* Grand Rapids: Zondervan Publishing House, 1974.

Larsen, B. *The Rational Revolution.* Waco, TX: Word Books, 1976.

Larzelere, R. E. "The task ahead: Six levels of integration of Christianity and psychology." *Journal of Psychology and Theology,* 1980.

Lewis, C. S. *Miracles.* London: Collins Fontana Books, 1947.

Lieberman, M. A. and Borman, L. D. (eds.) Special Issue: "Self Help Groups." *Journal of Applied Behavioral Science, 12,* 1976.

Lindsell, H. *The Battle for the Bible.* Grand Rapids: Zondervan Publishing House, 1976.

Lloyd-Jones, D. *Conversions: Psychological and Spiritual.* Downers Grove, IL: InterVarsity, 1959.

Malony, H. N. "Psychotherapy: Where the rubber hits the

road." Mimeographed, Fuller Theological Seminary, Pasadena, CA, 1978.

McQuilkin, J. R. "The behavioral sciences under the authority of Scripture." Paper presented at Evangelical Theological Society, Jackson, MS, December 30, 1975.

Meehl, P., et al. *What, Then, Is Man? A Symposium of Theology, Psychology, and Psychiatry.* St. Louis: Concordia Publishing House, 1958.

Montgomery, J. W. (ed.) *Demon Possession.* Minneapolis: Bethany Fellowship, 1976.

Mowrer, O. H. *The Crisis in Psychiatry and Religion.* Princeton: Van Nostrand Reinhold Co., 1961.

————. "What is normal behavior?" In *Introduction to Clinical Psychology.* E. A. Berg and L. A. Pennington (eds.). New York: Ronald Press, 1954, pp. 58-88.

Myers, D. G. *The Human Puzzle: Psychological Research and Christian Belief.* New York: Harper & Row, 1978.

Narramore, B. "Perspectives on the integration of psychology and theology." *Journal of Psychology and Theology, 1,* 1973, pp. 3-18.

Oates, W. E. *The Psychology of Religion.* Waco, TX: Word Books, 1973.

Oden, T. *Contemporary Theology and Psychotherapy.* Philadelphia: Westminster Press, 1967.

Pascoe, J. P. "An integrative approach to psychological and Christian thought based on a Christian world view." *Journal of Psychology and Theology, 8,* 1980, pp. 12-26.

Perri, M. G. and Richards, C. S. "An investigation of naturally occurring episodes of self-controlled behaviors." *Journal of Counseling Psychology, 24,* 1977, pp. 178-83.

Rambo, L. "Evangelical psychology." *The Christian Century,* December 28, 1977, pp. 1229-30.

Rogers, W. R. "The dynamics of psychology and religion: Teaching in a dialogical field." Paper presented at the Society for the Scientific Study of Religion, Chicago, October, 1977.

Salk, J. *The Survival of the Wisest.* New York: Harper & Row, 1973.

Sall, M. J. *Faith, Psychology and Christian Maturity.* Grand Rapids: Zondervan Publishing House, 1975.

Sargant, W. *Battle for the Mind.* London: Pan Books, 1957.
———. *The Mind Possessed: A Physiology of Possession, Mysticism and Faith Healing.* Philadelphia: J. B. Lippincott Co., 1974.

Schaper, R.N. "Complementarity and integration." Mimeographed, Fuller Theological Seminary, Pasadena, CA, 1978.

Selye, H. *Stress Without Distress.* Philadelphia: J. B. Lippincott Co., 1974.

Skinner, B. F. *Beyond Freedom and Dignity.* New York: Alfred A. Knopf, 1971.
———. *Science and Human Behavior.* New York: The Free Press, 1953.
———. *Walden Two.* New York: The Macmillan Co., 1948.

Smith, C. R. "What part hath psychology in theology?" *Journal of Psychology and Theology, 3,* Fall 1975, pp. 272-76.

Stackhouse, Max L. "On the boundary of psychology and theology." Paper presented at the Northeast Regional Convention of the Association of Clinical Pastoral Educators, Waltham, MA, July 19-20, 1974.

Sutherland, P. and Poelstra, P. "Aspects of integration." Mimeographed, Biola College, La Mirada, CA, 1979.

Thielicke, H. *The Evangelical Faith.* (Vol. I). Grand Rapids: Eerdmans Publishing Co., 1974.

References

Tillich, P. *Systematic Theology.* (Vol. I). University of Chicago Press, 1951.

Tournier, P. *A Place for You.* New York: Harper & Row, 1968.

———. *To Resist or To Surrender.* Richmond: John Knox Press, 1964.

Van Leeuwen, M. S. "The view from the lion's den: Integrating psychology and Christianity in the secular university classroom." *Christian Scholar's Review,* vol. 5, 1976, pp. 364-73.

Vitz, P. C. *Psychology As Religion: The Cult of Self-Worship.* Grand Rapids: Eerdmans Publishing Co., 1977.

Weber, T. "Coincidence of opposites: The meeting of psychology and theology." Mimeographed, Fuller Theological Seminary, Pasadena, CA., 1978.

Westberg, G. E. and Draper, E. *Community Psychiatry and the Clergyman.* Springfield, IL: Charles C. Thomas, Publisher, 1966.

Whitlock, G. E. *Preventive Psychology and the Church.* Philadelphia: Westminster Press, 1973.

Index of Subjects

Index of Names